I was riding the train to work one early December morning, my journal propped up in my lap. The snow clouds had gathered and pushed a cold wind and some snowflakes from the sky. My routine of journaling on my way to and from work was interrupted this morning when I looked across the aisle to see a man and a woman with two girls, laughing and talking. The older girl, about nine or ten years old, and her sister about four, were dressed up in Sunday clothes eagerly looking out the windows.

Their happy faces filled me with loneliness and grief. Were they going shopping or perhaps to see Santa Claus in the big department store downtown? I envied their togetherness, their obvious love for each other, their family circle.

I looked at my journal, the words swimming in the tears that fell on them. I had just been writing about my family—my parents, my sister.

The snow was now falling in a steady stream of white. I looked at my feet and was happy to have worn my boots today. They will keep me warm. I had been writing about a time during a winter when I was a little girl and had no shoes.

The store windows we passed were filled with Christmas decorations, and the houses had lights strung under their roofs. I thought now of all the wonderful holiday times with my family and friends. I wanted to get into the spirit of the season, to enjoy the sights around me, but I had been writing about Christmases long ago without family, without the usual Christmas Mass, without any celebrations or gifts.

I put away the journal for today. There would be other days when I would continue to fill the pages of the journal with my innermost feelings and the memories I was desperate to preserve.

I had to be thankful to be alive.

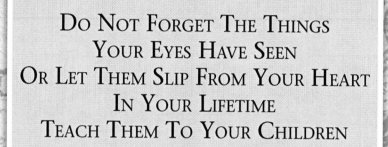

Do Not Forget The Things
Your Eyes Have Seen
Or Let Them Slip From Your Heart
In Your Lifetime
Teach Them To Your Children

Deuteronomy 4:9

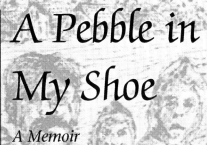

A Pebble in
My Shoe

A Memoir

Katherine Hoeger Flotz

Katherine Flotz

Pannonia Press
P.O. Box 1062
Palatine, Illinois 60078-1062

Printed and designed by Active Graphics Inc.
Chicago, Illinois 60607

Cover Illustration by Matthew Sesek.

Library of Congress 2004095421
ISBN 0-9657793-3-5

Printed in U.S.A.

DEDICATION

To our children,
Peter, Heide Marie, and Katherine Ann

To our grandchildren,
Daniel Paul, Lynne Marie
Clayton George
Cole Bates and Marin Katharine

To all future generations of the
Flotz Family

Foreword

by Charles M. Barber

Professor of History–Emeritus
Northeastern Illinois University

Almost every nation or Empire in history has at least one minority to put its capacity for tolerance to the test. The record is not encouraging, especially in the awful 20th Century, the era that has bequeathed to us the terms "genocide" and "ethnic cleansing."

On the other hand, we have the statement by Dr. Martin Luther King Jr.—a descendant of millions of victims of genocide and ethnic cleansing[1]—that "suffering is redemptive." In the case of Katherine Hoeger Flotz and her husband George, this is almost palpably true. They were redeemed in their own lifetimes, and in the United States, the land that saw the breaking of Dr. King's body, but neither his spirit, nor that of his people.

Our faith in suffering as redemptive is tested more sorely, however, when we are faced with the less fortunate victims of the *Vertreibung* [Expulsion][2]—that massive act of revenge for Hitler's crimes from 1944–1950 that claimed an estimated 14 million plus German-speaking peoples as brutally abused refugees, with around two million of them killed.[3]

The "crime" of Katherine Hoeger and George Flotz was to be who they were, not what they had done, the same "crime" foisted upon so many minorities in history—Jews in Christian nations like Hitler's Austria and Germany, 1933–1945, or the Spain of Ferdinand and Isabella in 1492; Christians in a Muslim nation, like the Armenians in World War I Turkey; Muslims, like Kossovars in Christian Orthodox Serbia, Palestinian Arabs in Zionist Israel, or, again, in the Spain of Ferdinand and Isabella; Protestant Czechs defeated by the Catholic Habsburgs; Catholic Irish defeated by the Protestants Oliver Cromwell or William of Orange; prosperous, hard-working peasants in Lenin's and Stalin's Soviet Union—the list is a long one.

One of the obligations of contemporary historians, in my opinion—especially those of us who have not suffered such oppressions —is to stare into the abyss of the Expulsion, the Holocaust, and the other ghastly ethnic cleansings sanctioned by the likes of Hitler, the Japanese Imperialists, Lenin, Stalin, Mao, Slobodan Milosovich, and, sad to say, the darker aspects of U.S. Domestic and Foreign Policy. As a recent volume on the subject makes abundantly clear, ethnic cleansing was, and is, an equal opportunity employer.[4]

Historians are especially in the debt of those survivors of the abyss, who have summoned the courage, either immediately thereafter, or later in life, to set down their stories. These survivor memoirs are absolutely crucial in giving context and meaning to the mind-boggling numbers of those who could not and cannot testify by dint of being dead or rendered speechless by the horror. Though it is especially poignant to have an expulsion narrative in which the protagonists tell their stories on their way to becoming husband and wife, this happy ending should not be allowed to obscure the nightmares that attended the expulsions of Danube Swabians like the Hoeger and Flotz families. To her great credit, Katherine Hoeger Flotz honors the memories of those who suffered more fully than she with her metaphor of a pebble in her shoe, rather than a more thoroughgoing, destructive one. Part of this, no doubt, is due to her personal honesty and integrity. Another part, perhaps, is due to a realization that, terrible as it was, Tito's ethnic cleansing lessened in intensity after the first few years, as Soviet occupation and Partisan revenge gave way to new realities of the Cold War. The testimony of one of Tito's closest collaborators and later antagonist, Milovan Djilas,[5] gives us insight into a Communist Yugoslavia in ever-growing conflict with the Soviet Union, that could ill afford to continue to overtly decimate its German-speaking population, when it would need tacit, if not open support from the West. Better to let the remaining Danube Swabians find their way out of the concentration camps of Gakowa and Rudolfsgnad and into refugee camps in Austria and Germany, than to continue to hound them to their deaths with so many German-speaking relatives in the countries of West Germany, Great Britain and the United States that were becoming increasingly important in Tito's survival strategy for his nation.

Thus Katherine Hoeger and George Flotz moved into the zones of freedom in Austria and Germany and became part of the economic miracle there. They and hundreds of thousands of their fellow *Volksdeutsche* and *Reichsdeutsche* refugees formed a fortuitous, skilled labor force that worked mostly for food and shelter only, and picked up the rubble from World War II in the late 1940's. They thus contributed mightily to the economic resurgence of Austria and West Germany in the early 1950's that continues today as the underpinning of the colossus known as the European Union. They then moved on to enrich the United States as part of yet another wave of German-Americans in the 1950's to match the earlier waves of German-speaking settlers of the 1920's, 1880's, 1850's, and earlier —accounting for well over 20% of the national population, the largest ethnicity in the United States.[6] That many of them, like George Flotz, came along just in time to fill draft quotas for the Korean War period was a rite of passage that has been little explored in U.S. Congressional motivations allowing for their entry at a time when others were being excluded.

George Flotz chose to look on the bright side of his duty to serve his new country, while his father was aghast—a fascinating part of this well-told and engrossing tale. Both he and Katherine clearly realized that the journey from being in the wrong place at the wrong time to the right place at the right time had more to do with the bright side of the promise of America than with its darker and less elevating chapters.

Charles M. Barber
Mandan, North Dakota
Professor of History-Emeritus
Northeastern Illinois University

ENDNOTES

1. Stephen Behrendt, "Transatlantic Slave Trade," *Africana: The Encyclopedia of the African and African American Experience*, New York: Basic Civitas Books, 1999, 1865–1877.
2. Alfred M. de Zayas, *Nemesis at Potsdam: The Anglo-Americans and the Expulsion of the Germans*, London: Routledge & Kegan Paul, 1977, 268 pp.
3. Alfred-Maurice de Zayas, *A Terrible Revenge: The Ethnic Cleansing of the East European Germans, 1944–1950*, New York: St. Martin's Press, 1994, 179 pp.
4. Vardy & Tooley, eds., *Ethnic Cleansing in 20th Century Europe*, New York: Columbia U. Press, 2003, 860 pp.
5. Milovan Djilas, *Conversations With Stalin*, New York: Harcourt Brace, 1962, 211 pp.; Wartime, New York: Harcourt Brace, 1977, 470 pp.; *Rise and Fall*, New York: Harcourt Brace, 1983, 424 pp.
6. Don Heinrich Tolzmann, *The German-American Experience*, New York: Humanity Books, 2000, 15 pp.

North Carolina State University is a land-   **Department of Chemistry**
grant university and a constituent institution
of The University of North Carolina

NC STATE UNIVERSITY

College of Physical and
Mathematical Sciences
Campus Box 8204
Raleigh, NC 27695-8204

"A Pebble in My Shoe"
A memoir by Katherine Hoeger Flotz

From March 1945 to February 1948 Gakowa and Kruschiwl were communist Serbia's northernmost extermination camps housing its indigenous Germanic civilian minority. For approximately 200 years this minority and its land were part of Hungary or Austria-Hungary until 1919, when WWI allies in the Treaty of Trion gave that part of southern Hungary (districts of Batschka and Banat) to Yugoslavia without plebiscite.

The author, Katherine Flotz, presents in her book with dynamically flowing narrative her earliest peaceful and orderly childhood (to age 8) in her native Gakowa. Then followed the Russian occupation (November 1944) and subsequent communist Serbian takeover under Marshall Tito's command. She describes the initial disaster when their able-bodied men and women were gathered up in cattle rail cars and shipped to the Soviet Union. This was also done in my town of Apatin and any other village containing ethnic Germans. Protests were ineffective because Tito declared our minority's citizenship void.

Mrs. Flotz then describes the next stage in the shocking developments of her Gakowa. In March 1945 Serbian communist guards were stationed around the village while huge numbers of ethnic Germans from other Batschka villages/towns were marched into Gakowa as well as into Kruschiwl 5 km north. These refugees were primarily old men and old women, younger women with children, but almost no young men, as the latter were already shipped to slave labor camps in the Soviet Union or had been drafted by the occupying German military. Our family (I was nearly 8 years old) and nearly all our relatives from Apatin were among those marched into Gakowa or nearby Kruschiwl in March 1945. As does the author, I too remember sleeping on a straw layer and blanket on the floor, people packed nearly elbow to elbow, fleas and lice rampant in the crowded conditions, the community kettles of watery soup with a few hard peas served each person in the long line, puss blisters on our arms from malnutrition. The author also describes the devastation brought by typhoid fever, of which her own mother and thousands of others died. Without medication some nevertheless survived; the author, my mother, and myself were among the lucky ones. The second most serious disease was malaria, and my little brother and grandmother were among the survivors of that. Of course no medications were made available by the Serb authorities, as extermination was their goal for us.

The author describes another constantly feared Serb guard procedure: the forceful removal and deportation of children whose guardians were other than the mother when they came for searches. The guards did this knowing full well that the younger mothers of children were required to work the fields during the day, with kids left with older women. This nearly happened to my younger brother and me, but our mother returned in the nick of time. In Gakowa we too were forced to witness rifle executions by guards of some mothers caught trying to escape the camp the previous night in order to beg at nearby farms for morsels of food for their children.

Eight of our older relatives died in Gakowa and Kruschiwl due to starvation, despair, typhoid, and so on, and were given their last ride on the daily morning death wagon, stiff corpses bundled up in their own clothing and carried to mass graves just as described by the author. Finally by 1947 the Red Cross exerted pressure on Yugoslavia's Tito to dissolve these extermination and slave labor camps filled with innocent civilian Germans. It then became possible, if you still had any valuables left (shoes, coat, money,...), to escape by first giving what you had to the "escape guide", who in turn had to deliver the goods to the camp commandant and guards. When the night guards changed, by pre-arrangement they became inattentive for about 10 minutes, during which time a small group with a guide left the camp and worked their way to the Hungarian border crossing. Our family did this in March 1947, while the author and her family crossed the border in October of that same year. The author's description of fleeing through Russian-occupied Hungary was similiar to our experience, but we headed for Austria by way of St. Gotthardt in western Hungary, while she and her group went to Germany. Her little sister fled Gakowa later with her aunt Barbara, uncle Anton and grandmother.

I found many parallels between the age 12 Katharine in her new "home" in Ludwigsburg in Germany and my age 10 life in our new "home" in Kapfenberg, Austria. Because there was no schooling in the concentration camp, we were older than our school class peers. We each encountered a new local Germanic dialect, food rationing, bigger towns than our birthplaces Apatin and Gakowa, difficulty trying to fit into the new societies, and seeing many bombed-out buildings in our new host cities. No bombing had taken place in Gakowa, or in Apatin even though it was on the Danube. Her family's thrill at receiving their immigration papers to the USA reminded me also of the same emotion when our papers arrived in 1952.

The book offers the reader a double bonus in that it also describes the plights of the then young George from Bezdan, later to become the author's husband in Chicago. His ordeals are well narrated and of special interest, because he fled from one communist region into another, ending up being shipped back to Batschka after the first try. However, his second attempt at flight was successful so that he ended up safely in Vienna. It seems that he lived through two lifetimes when all the actions are considered.

Looking back at the larger picture of post-WWII from 1944 to 1948, the Gakowa, Kruschiwl and other Yugoslav extermination camps, along with the similar anti-German actions in Czechoslovakia, Poland, Rumania, Hungary, etc. were all part of the largest "ethnic cleansing" of a civilian population in human history. This action was decided upon at a meeting in Potsdam by Churchill (representing democracy), Roosevelt (representing democracy), and Stalin (representing tyranny). This devastating decision at Potsdam displaced 15 million ethnic Germanic peoples between 1944 and 1948 and thereby dispossessed them of all properties. At least 2,100,000 of them were murdered or died of diseases or from starvation in concentration camps such as Gakowa and Kruschiwl. During a recent German-American Day gathering in Washington, DC, President George W. Bush acknowledged that the above described displacement of 15 million Germans was the largest "ethnic cleansing" in human history. Very few Americans are aware of this. Katherine Flotz's "A Pebble in My Shoe" can help spread the word that innocent Germans suffered too in extermination camps, even into peacetime up to 1948.

Every public library should also acquire this very well written factual book, since it describes a representative example of the largest "ethnic cleansing" in human history.

Sincerely,

Anton Schreiner
Professor (Emeritus)
North Carolina State University
Raleigh
May 8, 2004

Dachau, Buchenwald, Gakowa, ...

Gakowa? What is Gakowa doing on this list? The first two are household words; few weeks go by without at least one of these being mentioned in the US media in connection with a survivors' story, a film, a play or some other 'holocaust' story. As important as it is to tell the story of Buchenwald and Dachau it is also important to realize that these stories are only a part of the holocaust history. Gakowa and the other six of Tito's concentration camps are also a part of the holocaust story; a part that has not been covered at all by the US media.

With this book Kathy Flotz (nee Katharina Hoeger) will help to fill this huge gap by telling her story as a survivor of concentration camp Gakowa. I am also a survivor. Kathy and I are the same age and are second cousins. We both escaped after three years of internment from 1944 to 1947. From age 9 to 12 we had no opportunity to go to school, to get medical treatment for illnesses, to get eye glasses repaired or replaced, etc. etc. I was seriously nearsighted, so when my glasses broke in 1944, I had no choice but to go without them. But these were all minor problems.

The major problem was simply to survive. The food provided us by the camp was inadequate; it consisted primarily of 'soup' containing little besides water. People who did not find a way, by whatever means, to supplement the food rations provided, simply starved to death. Many thousands are buried in mass graves next to the old cemetery.

I had one enormous advantage over Kathy: parents. She was an orphan. My father, although he only had six years of schooling, typical for Gakowa, spoke three languages: German, Serbo-Croation and Hungarian. This helped him get on the crew that brought supplies in for the camp's commandant. Every day this crew took a train wagon, which they powered with their hands and feet, 20 kilometers to Sombor, the nearest town, for supplies. This gave my father an opportunity to smuggle in enough food to keep us alive. Also we received some help from Serbian friends in nearby towns. Serbs were free, only ethnic Germans were interred. The sole criterion was your last name. My grandmother was put in concentration camp but her female relative whose married name was Geszi was free because Geszi was judged to be Hungarian.

Another reason for my survival was the fact that Gakowa, the village of my birth, was chosen by Tito as a sight for one of his concentration camps. In 1944 ethnic Germans were forced out of their homes and marched from nearby villages into Gakowa. We were also forced out of our homes and the whole village of about 3000 people was put into a few houses in the center of town. But after a week or so we were allowed to go back into our own house but we could only use one room; the others were occupied by people from other villages about 20 to 25 people to one room. Straw was put all around the room, some blankets put on it and people slept next to each other on these blankets all around the room.

Many people between the ages of 16 to 35 were taken by cattle trains to work in Russian labor camps. My parents managed to avoid this fate, my father probably because he was a member of the above mentioned crew; my mother because, when she was chosen to go, had the courage to risk her life by sneaking away. My cousin John Weber, second cousin Tobias Brandt and many others were not so lucky. They spent 5 years, from about 1945 to 1950, in Russian labor camps. They survived and are, at the time of this writing, living in the Chicago area. To give the reader some idea of the conditions these people lived in I just mention that John Weber did not remove his shoes for two years: they slept in their clothes, including shoes, for warmth.

To supplement Kathy's story I mention just a few of my vivid memories from concentration camp Gakowa. These memories can be described as 'snapshots'. They are the memories of a 10 year old living under extraordinary conditions. These conditions were so bizarre that they are virtually impossible to comprehend by anyone who has not had similiar experiences. These snapshots are listed below in random order.

1. A few days after all Gakowa families were forced out of their homes and placed into a few houses in the center of the village, two of us 9 year olds snuck out of these guarded houses and roamed through the vacated houses. These houses had all been looted; the cows, horses, pigs, chickens, dogs, cats, etc were roaming freely. We saw a sow lying in a bed in a room!

2. After we were allowed to go back to our houses to occupy one room and the other rooms were given to the internees from other villages, the animals disappeared very quickly, yes including the cats and dogs. I remember seeing people dig up a buried pig and bartering for parts of it.

3. A latrine was constructed behind our house in some bushes; it consisted of just a long narrow trench with a plank over it that people could sit on. I remember when some friends and I hid in the bushes behind the latrine and waited for some women to come use it. We then shot at them with a sling shot.

4. An acquaintance showed us the scar on his head where he had been shot, somehow he survived. My neighbor, who was a couple of years older than I, was not so lucky. He died from his wound.

5. Gakowa was guarded by Tito's partisans, who encircled the village. My friends would sneak out at night to go begging for bread in the neighboring villages. I looked upon this as an adventure and begged my parents to let me go with them. But my parents would not let me go. Thanks to my father we were not as desperate for food as the families of most of my friends, for reasons explained above. Kids would go begging for obvious reasons: they were much more likely to get some bread and, if caught by the guards, the punishment would likely be less severe.

6. Nevertheless, against the strict orders of my parents, I left the camp four times; all in daylight with a friend. We were caught twice. The first time we were marched through the center of town to see the commandant. He admonished us and then let us go. The second time we were not so lucky. We were severely beaten by the guards who caught us; I remember lying on the ground and being kicked with a boot. Then we were locked up in a back room of the house the guards lived in and ignored. We could hear the guards in the front room playing cards, drinking and laughing. Occasionally one would go past our room to the outhouse in back. But they all kept ignoring us. After several hours we got thirsty, hungry and very restless. There was nothing in this room and the floor was a dirt floor. Somehow using

stones we managed to remove the glass from a window and escaped. I can vividly remember how scared we were and how fast we ran to get away.

7. When the town crier marched along the main street through town, this was the signal for all people to assemble on the soccer field. From this assemblage the commandant would choose the people to be sent to labor camps in the surrounding areas. After my mother had a narrow escape from the transport going to Russia, she refused to go to the soccer field, instead she would grab me and the two of us would hide, sometimes in the attic, other times in the bushes behind the house. This was always a very exciting, dangerous, and very scary time.

8. After the first year, various diseases such as typhoid fever and malaria broke out. There was no medical treatment of any kind, no medicine. On one occasion the block that our house was on was chosen to house the typhoid patients. Our house was U-shaped with one leg of the U shorter than the other; we were allowed to occupy the side with the shorter leg. On the other side were several rooms each occupied by 20-25 typhoid patients. There was a porch in front of these rooms all along the house. Every morning a few dead bodies were removed from the rooms, wrapped in a blanket and placed outside the room on the porch. I remember looking at these wrapped bodies every day during this period. A horse drawn wagon would come down the street; the bodies would be picked up and piled on top of each other on the wagon, then taken to the cemetary and buried in the mass graves.

9. We never managed to get rid of the lice. My grandmother, (bless her soul, if anyone deserves to be a saint she does,) would iron all our clothes, especially the underwear, but to no avail. The able bodied people were marched out into the fields to work, those too sick or too old to work, would lie around the front yard during the day and kill the lice with their finger nails. When they stopped killing lice it was a sign that they had given up on life.

10. Three years without school gave us children lots of time to play if we could stay healthy and avoid malnutrition. My

sister got very ill and came close to dying on at least one occasion. I can remember only one instance when I started hallucinating. This lasted a couple of weeks; I assume it was caused by malnutrition, but who knows? Fortunately this never recurred. Of course we had no balls or any other toys to play with. So we improvised. I remember at first we somehow go a hold of some pig's bladders to use for soccer balls but they didn't last long, so we played with balls made from rags.

11. If you are a smoker and want to quit but find it difficult to do so, I know a sure fire way: Get placed in a concentration camp. For a while smokers tried to improvise: dried grape leaves worked well but they soon ran out, some tree roots served as powerful cigars. After a few weeks there were no smokers among the inmates.

12. I remember guards walking along would suddenly, and for no apparent reason, take out a whip and whip an old lady.

13. My 15 year old sister hiding in a large earthen oven.

An atrocity is an atrocity whether it is committed during war or peace. However, in peace time we normally expect justice to prevail. The old lady who got whipped for no reason, the people who got raped, murdered, maimed, had no recourse. There was no police to turn to, no judge, and no jury. The commandant was all of these and more. The partisan guards were accountable only to him and him only, and to those above him who were far away and not concerned.

The events described above, these 'snapshots', occurred between 1944 and 1947. Although the camp was started technically before the end of World War II, during all but the first few weeks, it was run during 'peace' time. Yet, no one has ever been held accountable for the atrocities committed in the concentration camp Gakowa or any of Tito's other six such camps. In fact, it was only recently, since the fall of Milosevic, that the very existence of these camps has been publicly admitted and a modest memorial plaque has been placed to mark the mass graves. When I visited Gakowa in 1974 and, again in 1989 cows were grazing on top of the mass graves and there was no memorial of any kind.

Imagine Germany denying the existence of Dachau and Buchenwald! Yet, until quite recently, the former Yugoslavia denied the very existence of concentration camp Gakowa and the others. A denial accepted by the United States State Department in spite of thousands of survivors including Kathy Flotz and myself!

Anton Zettl
Distinguished Research Professor Emeritus
Department of Mathematical Sciences
Northern Illinois University
DeKalb, Illinois 60115
zettl@msn.com

A DRAWING OF EUROPE (1938)

1. Bremen	6. Munich	11. Bucharest
2. Berlin	7. Prague	12. Sophia
3. Dresden	8. Vienna	13. Rome
4. Frankfurt	9. Budapest	14. Bezdan
5. Ludwigsburg	10. Belgrade	15. Gakowa

CHAPTER ONE | My Hometown, A Quiet Village

The train whistles a warning to announce its afternoon arrival in the town of Gakowa, Yugoslavia. I run across the street to welcome the large, black monster powering towards me. At 8 years old, I find it exciting and fun to watch the "goings on" of the people getting off, unloading their baggage and greeting their families. Finally, the train moves on, and all is quiet again.

We live at the edge of town by the train station, on a corner lot. Chestnut trees line part of the house and an orchard of cherry trees graces the front of our living and bedrooms. My favorite fruit are cherries and I cannot wait for them to ripen. During the cherry-picking season, I sneak into the orchard and pick what I can from the low hanging branches. When a stomach ache follows because of my overindulgence, I suffer the consequences.

On the other side of the house is a huge garden. A white picket fence separates the garden from the black-tiled, covered gangway which runs along the inside of the fence. There are doors to the living quarters, the wine cellar and the *Wirtshaus* (tavern). Grapevines spin their way up the picket fence, reaching the roof. In the summer, the vines provide us with cool shade and luscious fruit. Vegetables such as carrots, beans, squash and beds of strawberries share their valuable space with flowers that beautify the garden. Running alongside the garden is our bowling alley. It has only one lane. The balls are made of wood and fit into the palm of a man's hand. The pins are set manually by the neighborhood boys who want to make a little money. On Sunday afternoons in the summer, the men come to bowl. There is a lot of raucous noise as they wager and boast of their abilities to knock down the pins. That is usually the time my mother takes my sister Erna and me to visit the relatives.

My parents own a Wirtshaus, a large room with tables and chairs where townspeople come to enjoy a glass of wine, play cards on the weekends and discuss the news of the day. Occasionally, some guests getting off the train will enjoy a simple meal prepared by my mother. She usually cooks chicken goulash with dumplings and potatoes, or stuffed peppers and noodles, or sauerkraut and ribs. Homemade bread and a glass of good wine usually accompany her rib-sticking fare. When people are in a hurry, a serving of bacon and eggs, or a plate of smoked ham, sausages and cheese would do.

During the harvest season, my father is in the business of brokering livestock and grains. We have a large warehouse next to our home for the grains and a barn on the opposite side of the home for the livestock. There is a gate that opens onto the street and across to the railroad station, directly to the railroad cars. This is a large undertaking, and my father needs many hands to help guide the livestock into the cattle cars. There is always a lot of noise coming from the animals and the men who try to persuade them in the right direction. I love to watch this spectacle: contest of wills between man and beast.

My father is a busy man and has little time for his children. It is not the custom for the father of the family to play with the children. He must work and provide while the mother tends to the little ones. I cannot remember that my father ever held me on his lap. We have the mealtimes together and often talk and joke, but during the day and in the late evening, he sits and works on the books for the business. There are no adding machines, or typewriters in our house, so he must do everything manually. My mother helps him after we are in bed.

The majority of the townspeople make farming their livelihood. They live in town but their land is outside the town limits surrounding the area. Each family has inherited or bought acres of land and some have more than others. On the acres of land usually sits a *Salasch* (a small house)—inhabited during the summer

The Hoeger Family in 1944—Katharina, Erna, Katherine and Wendel.
This is the last picture taken as a family, before our father left for the war.

months by *Salaschleut*—workers who lease the land for a percentage
of the harvest. These are people who don't own any land outright.
The owners drive out to the Salasch with their horse drawn wagons
to help with the various jobs of the season. They plant the seeds in
the spring. Then when the weeds begin to grow between the rows
of corn, beets, hemp, sunflowers and potatoes, it takes a lot of man
power and hoes to remove them. There is no weed killer available at
the time and all labor is by hand. The hoeing also loosens the dirt to
absorb the moisture during the rainfall.

The town of Gakowa in Yugoslavia, about five kilometers south
of the Hungarian border, is occupied by people who arrived here
about 200 years ago from Germany. They were given land by the
Emperor of Austria, who owned this part of the country, and asked
to settle and cultivate it. During the Turkish wars and occupation,
the country was devastated, but finally, in 1718 the German and
Austrian forces under the command of Prince Eugene of Savoy conquered the Turks.

My mother often tells me stories about our ancestors, who came from the Alsace/Lorraine Valley in Germany to establish the town of Gakowa in 1763. They arrived in small wooden boats called *Ulmerschachtel*—(Ulm is the city from where they started and schachtel stands for box). They traveled on the Danube River because there were no roads going to this area. My great-grandfather, Phillip Hoeger, was a shoemaker. Many others, mostly farmers, carpenters, bricklayers, blacksmiths, cleared the land and dug ditches to drain the water which flooded most of the area. Many died from hunger and illness before any crops could be harvested. But they persisted and, finally, small houses were built and livestock multiplied, crops grew in abundance and provided for their livelihood. The houses had to be built according to the specifications of the plans provided from the Emperor's architect. Therefore, most towns and homes were similar in style and size.

I always like listening to those stories. They are better than fairytales. I cannot imagine how my ancestors managed through all their hardships and sickness in the cold of winter. I often dream about how I would have survived.

I was soon to find out.

Our street, called *Bahnhofstrasse*, was named after the train station. It has cobblestone sidewalks lining a dirt road for the horse-drawn wagons. It leads all the way to the cemetery and then turns right into *Hauptgasse*, the main street in town.

In the middle of town stands the church of St. Martin, the school, the town hall and some small businesses: a butcher shop, small grocery stores, a blacksmith, a cabinet maker, a few Wirtshauses with a dance hall for weddings and special Holiday celebrations. At the north end of town, the St. Anthony Chapel guards the entrance. Whitewashed tree trunks stand guard along the sidewalks.

My father's parents, Sebastian and Katharina Hoeger live with us. I call them *Oma* and *Opa*—the equivalent of Grandma and Grandpa. My maternal grandparents, Nikolaus and Julianna Brandt reside at the opposite end of town. I call them *Altmutter* and *Altvater* (old mother and old father).

My mother is very close to her family. She takes my sister Erna and me for weekly Sunday visits. It takes us about 45 minutes to walk through town to get to Altmutter's house. On the way, we pass the home of my mother's sister, Barbara. We call her *Baewibas*. The addition of *"bas"* to a woman's name is used by children and teens when addressing older women as a sign of respect. The men are addressed by adding *"vetter"* to their names. Baewibas is married to Anton Findeis, a widower with three children. They also have one daughter together. Her name is Barbara also.

A block away, lives my mother's brother, Michael Brandt, who is married to Justina Dschida. We call them Justinabas and Mishkavetter. They have a son named Tobias. Justinabas' parents immigrated to the United States around 1915 and live in Chicago.

Whenever I stay with Altmutter for a visit, I sneak away and run to the home of Mishkavetter and Justinabas. As soon as I get to their front door, which is very big, I cannot reach the door handle. I do the next best thing. I lie on the ground and call:

"Justinabas, open the door" through the crack at the bottom. Soon she comes running and lets me in. I love staying at their house.

One summer day, I ask Justinabas if I could bathe in the wooden tub they keep in the summer kitchen.

Julianna and Nikolaus Brandt and their daughter, Katherine, in Gakowa, 1926.
(Altmutter and Altvater and my mother, age 10.)

Seated from left is my grandfather, Sebastian Hoeger, myself and my cousin Katharina Gokl and my grandmother, Katharina Hoeger.
Standing from left is my father and mother, Wendel and Katharina Hoeger, my father's sister and brother-in-law, Julianna and Anton Gokl. Photo taken in 1938.

My uncle, Anton Findeis with his horses in his yard in Gakowa circa 1930's.

She reluctantly agrees by saying: "I first have to get water from the well, make a fire in the stove to heat it and then you can jump in."

"I will help you, Justinabas," I tell her.

As soon as she pours the water into the tub and I can see how deep it is, I refuse to get into the tub. Justinabas is visibly upset and reminds me of all the trouble she has gone through. Tobias is watching us and tries to help:

"Kaethi, I'll go in first and you can sit on my lap so you won't be all the way in the water."

I finally agree and step in but the whole experience is not as enjoyable as I thought it would be. Justinabas is mad at me for being such a baby.

Each house has a *Regenwasserbrunnen*—a cistern to catch the rainwater for doing laundry. There is a rim around the hole and a metal cover over it. It is usually located in the yard near the kitchen where the laundry is washed in a wooden tub and scrubbed on a washboard.

On one of my visits to the Brandts', I make a game out of jumping over the metal cover of the well, trying not to touch it. Cousin Tobias is sweeping the yard and warns me to be careful. The cover must not have been put on tightly, because as I jumped over it, the cover fell into the well—along with me! Without thinking, and in the arms of my guardian angel, I spread my arms and grab a hold of the rim of the well. The well is filled to the top with water, so I stay afloat.

"Tobias, help me, help me," I scream at the top of my lungs.

"I am coming," he calls, "see what happens when you don't listen."

He is at my side in a few seconds and pulls me out. I don't think I realize the seriousness of this accident, because my only concern is for my new red sandals, that are now totally wet. *This was the first miracle in my life.*

Altvater owns a vineyard at the outskirts of town. During the fall months, when the grapes ripen to their fullest, the whole family gathers for the *Weinlese*, the harvesting of the grapes. My cousins and I run up and down the rows of grapevines, chasing each other, picking the ripe fruit and letting the luscious pearls burst in our mouths. There is joyful singing and laughing among the adults while they carry baskets of grapes to the wagon to be transported to the house. There, Altmutter is cooking a big meal for all the helpers. Because there are so many of us, a long table is set up in the yard and the family gathers around it, enjoying good food and wine, happy conversation and good times.

During the winter months, in bad weather, I stay at Altmutter's house because it is closer to the school. The school is right next to the church in the middle of town. I am in second grade. We sit obediently on our benches and pay close attention to the teacher. No talking or moving around the room is allowed. We learn to read,

WEINLESE—the harvesting of the grapes in Altvater's vineyard in Gakowa.
Happier times in 1941.

After grapes are harvested—dinner is served in the front yard for all the helpers.
I am seated next to Altmutter.

write and do arithmetic on the small chalkboards on our desks. When I do well on my report card, my mother rewards me with liquorice sticks, the red kind, which are my favorite.

There are only a few children my age near our house. I often visit the neighbors, who are kind and generous to me. One family raises bees, so I am lucky to get some beeswax to chew. It is like chewing gum, only the sweet honey oozes from the wax down your chin. The other family has a lot of fruit trees, including an apple tree whose fruit ripens early in June. They let me pick from the branches hanging close to the ground. Another family shows me postcards from their relatives in America, and I am intrigued by the vastness of the city of Chicago.

My sister, Erna, is two years old. She likes to explore the house and the surrounding grounds. I often help watch her and even though I am six years older, we have a lot of fun playing together. She has a wooden rocking horse, some blocks with pictures that compose a puzzle, a doll and some doll clothes. Our mother is a seamstress, so there are a lot of scraps of material, empty spools and pieces of lace and binding to make doll clothes. We play while our mother sews. Our mother is a happy woman, who is friends with everyone and likes to do charitable acts anonymously. During special holidays in the year, the poor on our street find gifts of food she has left at their doors.

Usually during the time of advent, mother is especially busy sewing new clothes for us girls and for herself. She is generous with her talent and time and makes new clothes for the grandmothers, aunts and cousins too. While we are asleep, she sews the new doll clothes and little blankets.

Much work goes into the Christmas preparations. We help make gingerbread men, chocolate filled wafers, and butter cookies that will hang on the tree. The Christmas tree is not decorated until the day before Christmas Eve and is kept hidden in one of the unused rooms. The tree decorations are mostly all edible: candy, cookies and strings of popcorn winding around the branches. Small tapered candles in metal holders are perched on the edge of the branches and will be lit only when the Christmas Eve festivities begin.

Early on Christmas Eve, we have a visit from the *Christkindl*, who brings a sack of gifts for the good children and a sack of coal for the bad. Of course, we always say we have been good and receive our reward. The Christkindl (Christ Child) is usually portrayed by a neighbor- totally covered in a white garment, face hidden behind a veil- who comes to scare the daylights out of us. This is a great way to make sure we are good for at least one month before Christmas.

We also have *Sankt Nikolaus Day* celebrations on December 6th. My grandfather's name is Nikolaus. The whole family gathers at his house and Altmutter makes fish soup, a special delicacy for the adults, and bakes *Kipfel* for us children. The children put their polished shoes outside the door. While we eat, Altmutter quickly fills the shoes with candy and nuts. She then rattles some chains and claims to be Sankt Nikolaus, while we pretend to be scared. After a while, we run out and find our shoes filled with special treats.

Instead of celebrating birthdays, it is the custom to honor people on their "Namesday". We are all named after saints, particularly Katherine, Michael, Joseph, Mary, Theresa, Barbara, Anthony, Martin and many more. There are three "Katherines" in our house, my mother, grandmother and myself. The whole family gathers on November 25th each year—St. Katherine's Day.

During the winter months, usually the beginning of December, family and friends get together for the *Schlachtfest* (slaughtering of a pig). This time of the year is chosen because it is cold so that the meat will not spoil. The pig has been fed well through the year and renders a good supply of food for us. When the pig has been killed, the meat is cut up for many different uses. Sides of bacon are diced in small pieces and fried resulting in a supply of lard (fat) for cooking throughout the year. The fried pieces of bacon are called *Krive* and are a special delicacy. Some of the meat is ground up, seasoned and pushed through a casing by a sausage making machine. Hams and sausages then hang temptingly in the pantry—some to be smoked to prolong their use—others to be eaten fresh in the near future. When the work is done, everyone sits down to a dinner of *Beischl*, a stew-like dish with a sweet and sour sauce. Then some of the *Bratwurst*, liver sausage and headcheese are sampled. Fresh bread and homemade wine accompany the meal and plans are made where the next "Schlachtfest" will take place.

An annual religious, as well as recreational custom is the *Kirchweihfest* (the celebration of the dedication of the church). Our church is dedicated to St. Martin and that feast day falls on November 11th. We also have a beautiful chapel built in honor of St.

My parents, Katharina and Wendel Hoeger on their wedding day in 1933.
My mother was 17 years old. She made her wedding gown.

Anthony. His feast day is in June, so we celebrate our Kirchweihfest during the warmer time of the year. After the Mass, it is time for the children to visit the carnival set up for this occasion. Booths of gingerbread hearts, candies, and toys are lining the main street. The older boys and girls show their talent in winning at various games of chance. In the evening, the brass band plays for dancing until the early hours of the morning. It is the custom for relatives from other towns to visit on this feast and share in the celebration. A thorough cleaning of the house, stables and yard takes place in anticipation of the event. The outside of the houses are white-washed, the yard is swept clean, the floors scrubbed. Food is prepared and cakes and cookies baked for the arrival of the guests.

Weddings are usually celebrated during the winter months when the farming people have more time and the food is safe from spoiling. There is no refrigeration. I am asked in November 1941 to be a *Kranzljungfer*, a flower girl at my cousin's wedding.

The wedding invitations are made in person by the friends and relatives of the couple. The couple, themselves, invites the nearest relatives. Young men go from house to house with a bottle of wine, say their wedding invitation greeting and invite the guests to take a drink. When the wine runs out, the invited guests must refill the bottle.

On the wedding day, the groom, accompanied by the town's brass band, walks to the bride's home to pick her up. The procession of the band, the bride and groom, the parents and relatives and friends follow on the way to church. After the ceremony, a dinner is given in one of the Wirtshauses. Days before the wedding, preparations begin with baking the cakes, slaughtering a pig, some chickens and, if it's a big wedding, even a cow. Everyone brings dishes and cutlery, tablecloths and glasses. It is a feast that the whole family and some of the neighbors must help to prepare.

After the dancing and toasting comes to an end in the early morning hours, the wedding celebration is not over. The next day, the relatives and the couple's friends arrive at the bride's home to help open the wedding gifts and then finish off the rest of the food from the day before. It is often a three day affair before the celebration ends.

The traditions that had been brought to Gakowa by the colonists some 200 years ago are still a part of our lives. It is the bond that separates us from the other nationalities in this country.

CHAPTER TWO | *Spring 1944*

My sister and I are anxiously looking forward to Easter. "Should we make a nest for the Easter Bunny yet?" I ask my mother.

She looks at us smiling and explains: "We should wait a little longer for the grass to grow. You know the Easter Bunny likes to eat the soft, cool grass before he leaves the eggs and candies."

Easter morning we go to church. Afterwards, we meet our relatives to show off our Easter outfits. My school friends and I admire each other's bonnets and cannot wait to go home and plunder the Easter baskets. My mother has sewn us all new dresses and our bonnets are new as well. She looks at us proudly and sighs: "You girls look just wonderful!"

My father admires the new pink and white polka-dot dress I am wearing and watches Erna twirl around in her yellow organza dress.

Later in the day, the family sits around a large table set in the Wirtshaus and enjoys the home-cured ham with all the trimmings.

"Can we eat our colored eggs now?" asks my sister, as she reaches for the prettiest one.

"I'll do it, you are still too small to crack them open," I chime in.

Opa and Oma chuckle as they exchange knowing looks.

"It's best to be careful with egg shells, Erna, so let your sister do it."

My mother, Katharina and cousin Tobias Brandt and myself
during a vacation trip in 1939.

After dinner, we all enjoy the cream slices made especially by
Mami.

This year, the festivities are not as happy because of the constant
news of war and the approach of the battle front. I hear the adults
talk of war and the relatives who have been drafted. I am so happy
that my father is still at home but wonder how long it will be before
he is also called into the German army.

Many of the people from Gakowa are preparing to flee the town
ahead of the Russian invasion and go to Germany. Talk about Russians invading our town scares them. They pack up their wagons

My sister and I, 1944—the last picture taken in Gakowa.

and horses, and leave their houses, livestock and land behind. I cannot understand it because there is war in Germany too. My family cannot bear to leave everything, so we stay.

In September 1944, the dreaded letter from the draft board comes to call my 31 year old father into service. He departs on September 15th. He kisses my sister and me and holds us tightly. He hugs his parents and then my mother accompanies him across the street to the train station for their final goodbye. It is obvious that he does not want to leave us. My mother worries about him because at this stage of the war, there is no time for basic training. Draftees receive no uniform, just a gun and instructions to shoot the enemy.

My mother is a very religious woman, and promises to have a statue of the Blessed Mother put up in our church if our father returns from the war safely. She prays with Erna and me each night before bedtime for his safe return.

While my father is away, it becomes necessary for my mother to do some of his work in the Wirtshaus. Many of the neighbors come to help and discuss the news of the war and the threat of Russian troops. I listen and am frightened when I hear about all the terrible things they discuss. I hear words like "rape." I don't know what that means, but it sounds bad and the look on their faces confirms it.

"Mami, what will the Russians do to us?" I ask anxiously.

"Don't worry, Kaethi, I will be here to take care of you," she reassures me, but I know she is scared herself.

The harvest time has come and gone. The people who left Gakowa did not reap all their harvest, so others in the town were appointed by the town government to bring in the rest of the corn for the winter. The livestock that was left behind is cared for by relatives or neighbors. The pigs and chickens are taken by relatives into their houses, but the cows take up more room and are stabled in their old master's barn. The cows must be milked every day.

At school, the teacher talks about the different places where the war is being fought, trying to familiarize us with where our fathers might be fighting. She mixes in the geography lesson with the current events. It is a world in uproar!

CHAPTER THREE | *Our Worst Fears Come True*

It is early morning November 25, 1944. It is St. Katherine's Day. We hear the town crier, banging the drum that hangs around his neck, and the families go outside to listen to his announcement.

"Everyone is to assemble in the town hall square by noon today. Leave your doors unlocked," he shouts so everyone can hear. He is visibly shaken. He seems to know more than he is announcing to us.

The people huddle together and discuss this unusual situation; everyone has a different opinion. The towncrier moves along to the next block and we go back into the house. Oma and Opa gather their valuables and my mother takes off her earrings and wedding ring in order to hide them. We fear that the valuables will be taken away if we are searched. She also takes off my ear rings and those of my sister Erna because she wants to keep them safe. I see my mother go to the back of the garden and start digging a hole. Most people bury their valuables in their gardens.

"Kaetl, what should we take along?" Oma asks my mother, while she looks around the rooms in panic." We don't know how long we will have to stay."

"Oma, just dress warm and we'll take some food for the children," my mother answers. "I am sure we will be back before it gets dark."

My mother dresses us warmly with several layers of clothing. The November weather is still dry, but cold. Opa has checked the gates to the chicken coups to keep in the fowl. The rest of the house has to be left unlocked. We are ready and, along with the other neighbors, we walk to the town hall. The mood is somber. We don't know what to expect. From all the news that has come to town from the other areas, it does not look good. When we reach the City Hall, my mother looks for her parents, her sister Barbara's family and her brother's family. We stay together in a group.

As soon as everyone is assembled, the men in charge, who look like Russian soldiers, take the individual families inside, search them and take away any valuables and money. The others are kept waiting on the outside in the yard. When darkness sets in, the men and women are separated and taken to various homes close to the town hall. My mother, Oma, Erna and I are assigned to the Melcher home. My Altmutter and Baewibas and young Barbara are in a different house, and Justinabas is separated from all of us. The men are housed in other homes across the street from us. We are told to stay for the night. We are cramped together filling all the rooms of the house. We try to find a place to settle down for the night. My mother uses her coat to make a bed for Erna and we just sit on the floor. Most of the little children are crying and it is a long time before things quiet down. I can hear the adults whispering their prayers for our safety. There is no heat in the room but with all the people huddled together, it is bearable. There is only one "outhouse" to accommodate everyone. The only place to wash is by the well in the yard. We have a little food that we brought along, but what about tomorrow?

The next day some of the men and women are told to go and feed the livestock in the houses that have been left empty. They come back with the news that our homes have been plundered of our possessions. There is much vandalism in the houses—furniture has been set on fire, clothes and bedding torn up. A few dogs are found shot that wanted to protect their master's home.

We are forced to stay in this "prison" for one week. My three-year-old sister cries for milk and is not happy to be inside one room with so many people. My mother tries to comfort us as best as she can. It is a cold November, so everyone stays inside. We children get restless and tired of this imprisonment, but the mothers tell us to be good. The soldiers, gun-toting bullies, are guarding the doors of the house and I am afraid when I see them. They look mean and seem to enjoy being in charge. They are quite young, maybe 18 or 19 years old, this must be their first assignment.

Some of the women are ordered to set up a kettle in the yard where the food is prepared for all of us. It is a meager meal of vegetable soup and whatever else they could find in the owner's pantry. We have no dishes or utensils with which to eat. Whatever is in the house must be shared. The adults wait their turn to eat until after the children have been fed.

After one week, we are ordered to line up outside again and wait. A few people are chosen to work for the partisans, to cook, bake and care for the livestock in the town. The others are taken to a neighboring town, Kruschiwl, about five kilometers away. That was the beginning of the concentration camp for them. With the exception of the few workers and the captors, Gakowa is now a ghost town.

Luckily, my mother, sister and I are chosen to stay in Gakowa, in the doctor's home, to help care for the few people too sick to be moved. There is a young man, an elderly woman and a lady who just had a baby. The midwife of the town is also allowed to stay behind. We all feel lucky to stay in Gakowa.

Justinabas and Mishkavetter are both staying in Gakowa. Justinabas has been chosen to work in the bakery and Mishkavetter, because of his knowledge of the Serbian language, is working in the headquarters of the partisans. Their son, Tobias, however, has been taken to Apatin to work at the airport. Many other young able bodied men and women from Gakowa are taken there as well. Baewibas is part of the milking crew and their daughter, Barbara is also working in one of the bakeries. Antonvetter is among the workers taken away. My grandparents are among those taken to Kruschiwl.

"I am going to try to sneak out tonight and go back home to get a few things out of hiding," my mother tells the midwife. "Would you go with me?"

"All right, I'll go, but let's be careful not to get caught," the midwife cautions.

Late at night, after Erna and I are asleep, my mother and the midwife leave the doctor's house, sneaking courageously through the dark streets. She had hidden some valuables in our home, but she cannot find them and has to return with only a few pieces of clothing and some food. I am amazed the next morning when she shows us what she brought. The package includes some flour, potatoes, home made plum jelly and some lard. She shares the food with the others in the house. She also remembered a few small toys for my sister and me.

"Weren't you afraid?" I ask my mother. "You might have been shot, if any of the guards caught you."

"We were careful and watched for any partisans on guard duty," she comforts us.

On or about December 20, 1944, we are released to go back to our homes, and the people taken to Kruschiwl are also allowed to come back home. During the short stay in Krushiwl, my great-grandmother, Katharina Brandt, died of hunger.

We are happy to be back together with our family. We believe that the worst is over. Opa and Oma Hoeger and my mother repair and restore order to our home as well as they can and prepare for the Christmas holidays. Many of our neighbors share food and drink to make the best of the situation. My mother visits her parents and the relatives to check on how they are doing.

We have not heard from my father. The holiday is overshadowed by grief and worry about his safety. There are no gifts on this Christmas Eve. The Christmas Eve services at church are filled with worshippers. On this fateful night, Tobias returns from the town of Apatin with some of the other workers. They had to walk through the cold and snow about 20 miles. He was one of the last ones released among all those taken from Gakowa. On his way home, he passes the church and stops in when he hears music being played. He spots his mother in the back of the church. She jumps up for joy and embraces him, thanking the Blessed Mother for his safe return. They both remain until the end of the service and then hurry home to get Tobias some food and a good night's rest. Christmas had come to the Brandt family that night.

But only three days later, on December 28, 1944, my ninth birthday, the town crier again announces a terrible message:

"All men between the ages of 17 to 44 and women between the ages of 17 to 30 must assemble at the train station. They are to bring enough food and clothes for 20 days."

Women with children under four years old are exempt. Thank

God, my mother is among them. However, my cousin, Tobias Brandt, is 17 and must go. My aunt is inconsolable and she cries for days. It is uncertain where they are going, he is so young.

That day, 135 men and women are taken from Gakowa for this labor assignment.

The train leaves Gakowa and takes them to the nearest city, Sombor. Other trains arrive, filled with young people from the German towns in the area. They are loaded into cattle cars, 50-60 to a car, and taken to a place unknown to them. It is learned much later that they have been taken to Russian slave labor camps to work in coal mines and lime pits. The work day often lasts 12–14 hours with little nourishment. The winters are cold, especially in the depth of the mines and their clothing is not adequate. While working under these conditions, with guards always present and watching, it is harsh punishment for these men and women who have not committed a crime.

Marshall Tito, the communist leader appointed by Stalin to take charge of the ethnic cleansing of the Germans in Yugoslavia, did not waste any time. His guerilla fighters known to us as "partisans", took over after the Russians returned to their country victorious. Their cruelty had no bounds.

In March, 1945, we begin to see groups of people being marched into town, flanked by Tito's partisans, toting guns on their shoulders. The marchers carry bundles on their backs and look exhausted from their long walk. They are coming from German towns like Apatin and Filipowa in the Batschka region.

Although we are in our homes, we cannot leave Gakowa. We are still prisoners. The outskirts of town are now patrolled by the partisans. There is about 100 feet distance between each armed guard so there is little chance of anyone getting out. However, as time goes on and the pains of hunger increase, ways and means are found to get through. Since there is no barbed wire, one must wait for the guard to change, or the moon passing behind some clouds. After a few tries, the people find their own ways out, perhaps through high bushes, low lying areas or in the storms of the night. Many are caught, and then brought to the commandant's attention. He then imprisons them in the cellars of two larger homes on Main Street that used to belong to the owners of Wirtshauses in town. It is the place where they stored the wine barrels. Of course, the cellar is empty now—only fit for the victims of their crimes. It is dark, cold and has no facilities for washing or bodily functions. It has become unbearable from the stench. When the partisans are drunk and want some entertainment, they often find pleasure in beating some of the people, or raping the women. And yet, the practice of trying to escape to get food from Hungarian or Serbian people living near the camp never stops anyone. Some of the other nationalities that live nearby are kind and helpful to the beggars, but others are mean and drive them away with cursing and have their dogs chase them.

This is the beginning of the concentration camp Gakowa—the beginning of the end.

CHAPTER FOUR

Two Families—
Different Paths

D uring the turmoil and chaos in the fall of 1944, two families experienced the tragedies of the times in different ways.
One was mine; the other was the Flotz family from Bezdan,
whose son, George Jr. was to be my future husband. Bezdan is only about
ten miles from Gakowa, but we did not know each other.

While my family decided to stay in Gakowa, the Flotz family prepared to leave their home in the hope of finding safety in Germany. The
propaganda that the Russians were invading our land, raping, plundering
and killing, was enough to drive many families away.

Their father, George Sr. had been drafted into the German army in
September of 1944 at age 41. The Flotz family now consisted only of
mother Anna and three boys, Lorenz 14, George Jr. 12 and John 5. Oma
Flotz refused to leave home. She said that she was born here and would die
here, if necessary. She met with a harsh fate later on.

Since they had no wagon or horses of their own, they asked a relative
to take them along. It was agreed and they left on October 11, 1944.

George Jr. tells the story of their journey.

At twelve years old, I was not happy to leave my home, my
friends and all the familiar places that boys like to explore. I loved
going to the Danube River to watch all the ships go by. I dreamed of
one day working on a ship that would take me out into the world of
adventure. My Mom, however, a courageous woman only 5 ft. tall

The family of George and Maria (Roth) Flotz, and their children taken approximately in 1907. The boy on the right next to Maria is George's father.

with great determination was ready to take us boys on this journey. She felt it would be safer for us in Germany where we might be able to find my father. She packed up some clothing and a little food and told us: "We cannot take anything other than the bare essentials because we are taking someone else's transportation, so please help me pack up your clothes."

Mom knew that it would be a long and hard time before we reached our destination but she kept her fears from us.

"Can I take my toy wagon?" asked little Johnnie, holding it tightly to his chest.

"No, dear, that's impossible. We need to take your clothes."

But, to quiet him down, she relented and let him take a small wooden soldier.

My father had a blacksmith shop next to our small house. He often got paid in goods, rather than money, for his services. At harvest time, we would receive wheat or corn and some livestock to carry us through the winter. We had no horses or wagon of our own. While

The Flotz Family in 1944 before leaving Bezdan, Anna, Larry, George Jr., George Sr., and little Johnny.

packing up our things, I looked once more into the blacksmith shop. Memories of my father at the anvil, hammering the hot horseshoes to fit the hooves of the horses, came flooding back. Would I see this image again?

My brother Lorenz and I helped our mother feed the chickens and the pig one last time and got the house in order for our Grandmother. She insisted on staying home, and we could not persuade her to come along.

We packed our things in the wagon of our relative and started out early in the morning. It was five kilometers to the Danube River; we needed to cross to the other side to continue the journey. Because the road was congested with other refugees and the German army, it took us until dusk to reach the Danube. There was no bridge across the river, so the wagons were loaded onto a ferry, six wagons at one time. It was a cold and rainy day and we felt the dampness in our bones.

It had been a long and cold day and we were hungry. If that was not enough, once we reached the other side of the Danube, we

School picture from Bezdan, 1938. George Flotz is fifth from the left in the first row. His brother, Larry, is fifth from the right in the first row. Their friends, Joseph Stein, Franz Stigler, Stefan Erg, Maria Kaufman are also in the picture.

were told by the relative that they were not taking us any further. My mother did not tell us why, although, I was sure she knew. She cried as she huddled us together. We slept under the stars that frosty October night.

The next morning, the German soldiers in the area told us that they would take us along on their wagons until we reached a Hungarian town called Bacsalmas. We remained there for three days and then continued on to Pecz, Hungary, where the open market place held wagons and horses that had been confiscated by the German soldiers from the local farmers. During wartime, it was a law that if the soldiers needed anything, it was your duty to give it, under threat of imprisonment.

We were assigned a wagon and two horses and joined a convoy of 12 wagons. The lead wagon was instructed by the military which direction to take to Germany.

We had no more food and we could sleep only on the wagon or in a barn, if the farmers let us. We children begged for food whenever we arrived in a town or passed a farm. It was not hard to do when you are hungry. Sometimes the people were nice to us, other times they called out the dogs and chased us away. We often cried when this happened. We could not understand the cruelty of these people. We were so hungry.

While traveling down the congested roads with other refugees, we were often besieged by airplanes strafing the area. We jumped out of the wagon, hid under it or dove into the ditch by the road. Air attacks riddled the skies, the noise near us unbearable. My little brother John screamed with fear while we tried to calm him. We were all terrified for our lives. This was now a daily part of life for us. Some days, when the war raged above us, we could not travel at all, and the journey, especially for us children, was slow and tiring.

At the end of November, we arrived in a town called Sopron, where we surrendered the horses and wagon to the military. We were then put on a train that took us to Glogau, a town in Eastern Germany in a State called *Schlesien*.

For ten days, we lived in a gym with many other refugees. We slept on the floor on a bed of straw. We began to notice that we had lice in our clothing. They like to hide around your midriff under the belt. It became a daily ritual to look for and kill them.

By December 1944, we were on the move again because the

battle front was approaching. Because so many refugees roamed the countryside and towns, any available transportation was free to us. The German army helped arrange for the ways and means of travel, either by bus, train, or even horse-drawn wagons. We arrived at a small town, where we were housed in a room above the barn of the owner's home. We were given ration cards and a little money because my father was in the German army.

Food and supplies were distributed from a central location, a one hour walk from the place where we were staying. My brother Lorenz and I walked to the center in the cold December weather. We had little warm clothing and shivered while trudging across the snowy fields. We became used to the long walk, but the heavy load we had to carry back was a hardship for two undernourished boys.

We often went into the surrounding woods to gather firewood to warm our room. Once, we saw a small Christmas tree. Since it was close to Christmas, we cut it down for our little brother. We found small odds and ends to decorate the tree but had no presents to give each other.

On Christmas Eve, the farmer gave us a chicken for our dinner. This loving and kind gesture could have resulted in severe punishment. The farmer had been ordered to turn over all livestock and grain to the government.

While my mother was preparing the chicken, we heard voices outside. A truck with a couple of Hungarian soldiers had arrived. My mother spoke to them in their native tongue:

"Come in and warm up," she called. "Please share our Christmas dinner with us."

Shortly after we sat down to eat, there was a knock on the door, and a military commando told us to leave immediately because heavy fighting was very close by. After the Hungarian soldiers departed, we packed up our few belongings and made our way to the train station. We left the chicken dinner behind.

When we arrived at the train station, we were again among many women and children fleeing from oncoming fighting. Our destination was unknown as we boarded our train. The inside walls of the unheated train had frost on them, and as our warm bodies expelled heat, droplets of the melting frost fell on us and soaked our clothes. It was Christmas Day 1944, certainly no place to celebrate.

A few days later, the train arrived in Oschatz (Saxony). Again, we were assigned to a refugee camp in this small town and then transferred to the castle of a former nobleman, who had to open his home to the refugees.

The owner still lived there with his family and other relatives who came from the big city. We were lucky enough to be assigned to the servants' quarters on the third floor of the castle. Three other families from Bezdan, with whom we traveled, occupied the same apartment. One of the relatives of the nobleman was a lady doctor. She was very helpful to us—especially when diarrhea set in. We also had lice again, this time head lice. The nice doctor had some powder to eliminate these pests. I don't know what we would have done without her help.

One day, my mother decided we should all go to Dresden, the big city known for its beautiful *Frauenkirche*—the church of Our Lady, the museums and the sky-high buildings. Dresden had been spared and damage from the air raids was minimal. Since the war was near its end, the people of Dresden hoped the city would not be bombed. They were wrong.

February 13, 1945 was the infamous night of fire bombings. While we were sightseeing, the air raid siren went off, and we hurried to a shelter. Soon the "all clear" signal was given and everyone came out, but without further warning, the Allied Forces returned. They dropped flares to light up the city, and then dropped incendiary bombs by the hundreds. The city became a holocaust of flames.

"Children, come quickly, we must return to the shelter," my mother called as she grabbed little Johnnie by the hand.

I warned my mother to stop because the entrance to the shelter was burning. There was no way to get out of this inferno, except to dash between the flames.

We saw people dropping to the ground, grabbing their throats, trying to breathe. They were suffocating from the oxygen deprivation and burning alive as the cement sidewalks burst into flames. We ran between the flames and the people trying to escape this mass murder. I cannot explain what I felt—total terror and yet the iron will to run for my life.

The city zoo was also burning. Some animals had escaped and were running wild in the streets. It was total chaos. The emergency vehicles could not get through because of the fires. The animals were dangerous, even more in their panicked state. Thousands of lives were lost this day.

The beautiful Frauenkirche suffered the most damage. The city was in ruins, its crumbling walls blocking traffic. The injured were spiritually and mentally devastated. The next day, the bombings stopped, the fires burned out and the people calmed down.

Surprisingly, the train station was not totally damaged and we were able to leave the city by train and go back to Oschatz—thankful for our lives and certain in the knowledge that our guardian angel was at our side.

It was now late April 1945. We saw a Russian soldier on horse back approaching the castle yard.

"The Germans must have lost the war," one of the refugees said to my mother. "The Russians must be in power now."

Each day, more and more Russians arrived; they occupied the castle with the rest of us. They did not bother us because my mother speaks Serbian, which is close to Russian. But they plundered and destroyed the art works and furniture in the castle.

"You should go back home to Yugoslavia," the soldiers advised my mother.

We decided to wait and see.

In May, 1945, World War II ended. We decided to leave the castle, but not to go to our home in Yugoslavia, rather going to the American occupied zones of Germany. Our only possessions fit into a little wagon, now common these days; we pulled it by hand and walked to the West. There were hundreds and thousands of refugees on the roads looking for their families.

Days later, we arrived in Chemnitz, the stepping stone to the western part of Germany. Up to this point, we had been walking. In Chemnitz, we stayed at a railroad station, hoping for transportation. Early in the morning, while we children were sleeping, my mother saw a woman walking towards her that looked familiar. At first she thought she saw a mirage. Could it be Anna?

"Anna, is it you?" my mother called out and jumped up for joy.

"*Tante* Anna, where did you come from?" my mother's niece shouted.

Meanwhile, we boys woke up and heard the commotion. We all gathered around our cousin and exchanged hugs and greetings. My mother asked about her sister, Theresa, and Anna explained:

"We work on a farm just outside of Chemnitz. Why don't you and the boys come with me? My mother will be so happy to see you."

"We were planning to go to the American zone in Germany," my mother explained, "but I have not seen my sister and you since 1939, so we will join you."

My mother's sister and her family used to live in Krndija, Croatia. We had not been able to visit them because in 1941, our hometown of Bezdan, became part of Hungary and Krndija became part of Croatia. The border then separated us and it was difficult to get permission to cross over. Now was our chance to see each other again so my mother decided to delay her decision to go to the American zone.

"Let's get our things together, boys, and we'll go with Anna."

The walk was uphill all day and Johnny, who was only 6 years old, had a hard time keeping up. We boys were all tired and irritable but we finally arrived at the farm.

"Mother, look who I brought with me," shouted Anna.

Aunt Theresa, my mother's older sister, came running from the house, unable to believe her eyes. She could not stop crying—but they were tears of joy. Our cousin, Karl, who at 16 was already working on the farm, joined us later for supper.

"It's a gift from God to have found you, Anna," Aunt Theresa said while she wiped away her tears. "How did you ever find us?"

My mother looked up and smiled: "It's a miracle that Anna was walking by that morning."

My aunt and cousins only had one room in which they lived and slept. The only place we could stay was in the hayloft. We slept on the soft hay with a roof over our head. This was better than wandering around the country trying to find shelter. The farmer was kind enough to give us food and we, in turn, did some chores on the farm.

"Maybe we should go back home," Aunt Theresa told my mother. "Our husbands may have returned from the war by now."

About a month after we arrived on the farm, the two families decided to go home. We packed our things into the little pull wagon and headed for Dresden, the main rail connection to Yugoslavia.

In Dresden, we were reminded of the destruction, which was widely visible. Most of the buildings were in ruin and there was no drinking water. The odor of the fire bombs still lingered in the air. We slept under the canopy of a bombed-out gas station near the railroad, waiting for a train to take us back home. There were many other refugees waiting too. While we were asleep, someone stole our bag of important papers and photographs, our only proof of identity. The thief must have presumed valuables or money were in the bag, but the only value was to us; our identity was now lost, along with everything else.

A few days later, we boarded an open railroad car. There were about two dozen people in the car with us. In the next car were Yugoslavian soldiers, going home after being released from POW camps.

Our destination and travel itinerary was now controlled by the Communists. Some days we traveled; others we stood in railroad yards. During that time, my brother Larry and I went into the nearest town or to farms to beg for food; in desperate times we even stole.

But a few times the train took off without us, and we had to catch the next train to find our mother. We always caught up to her and Johnnie. Sometimes we were lucky to get some food, so my mother hurriedly made a fire by the side of the train tracks to cook it.

It is now June, 1945. I had a birthday on the 24th—my 13th birthday. We were still on the train.

The POWs took good care of us. When we arrived in Prague, hatred for the Germans was high. Some Czechoslovakian soldiers came aboard and asked: "Who is German here?"

My mother spoke Serbian and we children were warned to be quiet. The POWs, in their wisdom, told the soldiers that the women and children belonged to them. Although skeptical, they believed this and left us alone.

This train ride and lifestyle lasted ten weeks.

When we arrived in Pressburg, a town located in the southwest corner of Czechoslovakia near the Austrian border, we were evacuated from the train and our belongings were inspected. The Communist officials helped themselves to what they wanted, but we had very little. We had no money or valuables, merely a few pieces of clothing and some pots and pans. The rumors of Communism started to sink in. At this point, the POWs were separated from us and we never saw them again.

The journey continued heading towards Hungary and Yugo-slavia. Our lifestyle improved a little because it was summer and there were fruit trees and vegetable gardens from which to pick food whenever the train stopped.

We finally arrived in Subotica in Yugoslavia. Guarded by Tito partisans, we were not allowed to leave the train. Outside, one of the partisans recognized my mother. He casually asked her to come behind the train. She feared the worst. But, he identified himself as a young man from our hometown, Bezdan, who had been forced to join Tito's army.

"Don't go back to Bezdan," he warns my mother. "All the Ger-mans are in concentration camps and their property has been con-fiscated."

Another angel in disguise.

On the pretense of arresting us, he took us off the train, and put us on another one going in the opposite direction—back where we came from in Hungary. My mother's sister and our cousins were still with us and were allowed to get off the train too.

In August 1945, we arrived in Baja, a town just across the bor-der into Hungary. The bridge across the Danube River had been de-stroyed. The Communists provided a pontoon to let the train cross. This was done at night during a fierce thunderstorm and we were riding in an open cattle car. When we approached the other side, the tracks from the pontoon bridge to the shore did not match, due to the rising water. We were stranded until dawn. Luckily, the cables connecting the pontoon held. By the next morning, help arrived and the train was able to proceed. We were soaked to the bones from the rain, but it was the only way we had to bathe.

CHAPTER
FIVE | # Concentration Camp Gakowa

W*e have received no news from my father and the war rages on, while we are imprisoned in our own town of Gakowa.*

It is mid April 1945. Warm weather washes over us, awakening our desire to plant seeds for another harvest. This food will supplement the meager rations. The residents of Gakowa can remain in their homes but must accept the daily influx of people being brought from other German towns. So far, no one has been brought to our house. I think the partisans have their eyes on it and want to make it their headquarters. They also know there are barrels of wine in the cellar of the Wirtshaus.

It is another day of watching the parade of old people and children march into town from their villages, weighted down with their belongings. The partisans alongside of them curse at them and hit the ones who are too tired to go on with the butts of their rifles. My mother and I are standing by the gate of our house, looking out at this sea of inhumanity. My mother is heart-broken at the sight of this sad picture. I see her wiping away tears.

One man steps out of line and asks my mother for a drink of water. She runs to our well and brings a cup of fresh, cool water for him.

"*Vergelt's Gott,*" (may God reward you) he whispers, while gulping it down. "We come from Apatin, where I just buried my wife.

She died of typhoid fever."

He quickly moves on to avoid the partisan's wrath. My mother is deeply moved and waves to him as he leaves. She takes my hand and we go inside the yard of our house. She walks back to the well and dips the cup in to get more water, takes a sip herself and then gives some to me.

A week later, my mother and I are in bed with a high fever. We are told that this is a symptom of typhoid fever. A rash forms on our bodies and we drift in and out of consciousness. There is a doctor in town, but he is helpless to treat this disease. He gives us a liquid medicine which he believes will help the high fever. My mother takes it willingly. I, however, press my lips together and refuse to swallow.

Altmutter has come to help take care of my mother and me. She takes turns with Oma and Opa Hoeger, who live with us, at our bedside. No one else can enter the house, because of the sign on the door warning of a contagious disease, so we have no other visitors. My mother and I are in separate beds but in one room. The curtains are drawn and the grandparents move quietly in and out of the room. My mother is concerned about my condition, but I am too young to understand the seriousness of our illness.

Sometimes I hear my mother's voice: "Kaethi, can you hear me? Are you in pain?"

But I cannot answer because I am in and out of consciousness. Sometimes I hear the whispering of the grandparents as they tend to my mother and explain to her how I am doing. This disease is very contagious, so my sister, Erna, is taken to the Findeis family, my mother's sister and brother-in-law. Even the partisans stay away because they, too, fear this dreaded disease.

During some of my conscious moments, I hear Altmutter crying: "My poor child is only 28 years old, and little Kaethi is so fragile."

All we can eat is some vegetable broth, so we slowly weaken from the high fever. I do take the broth, but as soon as the medicine is brought to my lips, and I taste the bitterness, my lips are sealed. I am refusing this help. I am a stubborn little girl.

The raging fever lasts twenty one days. On May 10, 1945, my mother dies of a hemorrhage. By the grace of God, I live. I hear a lot of crying and wailing in the room. Gently I am told that my mother has died. In my semi-conscious state, I hear the voices and through this haze I see my mother being carried out of the room. I can't believe that she is gone and I am still alive. I had always been sickly and frail, so how could I survive this disease. I lift my head slightly trying to see her one last time. She is moved to another room and prepared for burial. Because we are residents of Gakowa and have a family plot in the cemetery, it will be permitted to bury her properly in a wooden coffin. This practice soon stops due to the large number of deaths in the camp.

One of our neighbor ladies, *Frau* Herzl, sits by my bedside and tries to keep me calm. Outside, the funeral procession of family and friends is lined up as they carry the coffin to our cemetery for burial. I am too weak to comprehend or to cry. My sister, Erna, not quite four years old will take the place for both of us at the funeral. She, too, is unaware of the future hardships in our lives and those that must care for us.

Soon, my fever subsides and I begin to improve. The doctor tells us that the contagious period is over. We are very thankful that our grandparents, who cared for us, did not catch this fever. I am unable to eat solid food because my stomach has shrunk from the long period of fasting, so each day I am given a small piece of bread dipped in broth.

The weight I lost and the weakness from the fever prevents me from walking, and all my hair has fallen out. Slowly, each day, I hold on to the furniture or the walls around the room and practice walking like a new baby. Eventually signs of new growth promise a full head of hair in the future, and I am able to walk again.

Erna is brought back home to see me. She is not quite four years old and asks for Mami. She sits on my bed and we cry together, while I tell her that Mami is gone. I can finally accept the inevitable—we are now alone.

I try to comfort her. "Don't worry, Erna, soon our father will return from the war."

I had heard my grandparents talking that the war had ended early in May, while I was sick, so now I am full of hope that our father will soon return. Little do I realize that while the war in Germany has ended, the "fight for our lives" is just beginning.

The sign has been taken off the door, and soon the partisans come to inform us that we must leave the house because it is now their headquarters. It is the middle of June 1945. We are one of the few families in Gakowa that must vacate our house. We take what we can carry. Some of my clothes are packed up and a few things from my mother are included in the bag. When she was a young girl, my mother made a needlework picture of the crucified head of Christ. Oma wants me to keep that to help me remember what a devout woman my mother was. She also includes my report card from the last school year. I guess she feels I might need that one day. My Hoeger grandparents move to their daughter's house and take my sister with them. I am to go to the Findeis family, my mother's sister and brother-in-law, for recuperation.

Altmutter comes to pick me up and take me to Aunt Barbara's house. On the way, we will pass the cemetery. Since I have not yet been to my mother's grave, I ask Altmutter:

"Can we stop at the cemetery, and take some flowers to Mami's grave?"

"Yes, let's pick some flowers from your garden and take them along."

I hold Altmutter's hand as we walk down the Bahnhofstrasse towards the cemetery. Some of our neighbors come out to talk to us:

"Kaethi, how are you feeling? We hope you will get strong very soon. We'll miss you and your mother."

I cry a little as I say goodbye to some of my playmates. It is devastating to lose my mother and now I have to leave my home too. I am very sad as we continue on toward the cemetery.

"I'll always watch over you and Erna," Altmutter comforts me as she holds my hand tighter. She is heartbroken herself to lose a child so young, but she keeps telling me that we'll be alright.

"Altmutter, how can we find my mother's grave?" I want to know.

"When you enter the cemetery, there is a main walkway down the middle of it, and it goes up to a small hill. At the top of the hill, there is a cross and just to the right about two graves in, is your mother's grave," she explains.

As we enter the cemetery, we see other people coming to bury their loved ones. We begin walking up the hill and before we even get to the grave, Altmutter begins to cry. It is just too soon for her to forget her heartbreak. When we arrive, she is overcome with grief and cries uncontrollably while she places the flowers on the grave. I, too, am crying and we hold each other. This is the first time I am able to cry for my mother as I stand by her grave and finally realize she is gone.

"Don't worry, Kaethi, I will always watch over you and Erna," Altmutter assures me. "I promised your mother on her deathbed."

After our visit, we walk down Main Street, stop in the church to give thanks for my recovery, and eventually arrive at Aunt Barbara's home.

I am surprised to see so many people in the house. During my illness, many people from other towns have been brought to Gakowa. Each house has to take in as many as possible. There are at least ten people in the room—my aunt and uncle, cousins plus another family from Apatin, who are friends of my aunt.

"Come in, Kaethi, and put down your things over here," Baewibas invites me in. They all welcome me with smiling faces. I see that there are no beds, only blankets spread over straw on the floor.

"Thank you for taking me in. I am so tired from the long walk. Can I sit down somewhere and rest; I am still not fully recovered?" I ask them.

"Come over here, Kaethi, I have fixed a place for you to sleep," Baewibas leads me to one of the straw filled beds.

One of the women from Apatin, a lady of small stature with a slight limp, smiles graciously and tells me that she is a seamstress.

"I can alter some of your mother's dresses to fit you and your sister," she volunteers, just to make me feel better.

Since there is a strict custom of wearing black when there is a death in the family, all my clothes are dyed black. This will prolong my grief and be a constant reminder of my loss.

My recovery from the illness is slow. I cannot do much running or playing outside. I just sit and watch the other children while they play hopscotch or collect leaves and stones from the ground. Some of my school friends live nearby and they come to play with me. I still have a doll and some games, which Altmutter brought for me.

There are apple and pear trees in my aunt's garden and a small strawberry patch. It is summer of 1945 and we wait for the fruit to ripen. We don't pick the fruit until it is ripe, but we can eat what has fallen to the ground. Each morning, the children run to the garden to find the fruit which the trees have discarded. What a treat! The other fruit will be harvested and dried for the winter.

There is still some food left from the winter storage, so we share with the others in the room. Most of the furniture in the house has been removed to make room for the refugees and their belongings. The furniture is stored in a few of the houses designated for that purpose.

The cows left in the barn are milked by my aunt each day, but the milk must be turned over to the partisans. When she finishes milking, she always "loses" a little out of the pail and makes up the quantity with water. That's how we survive.

Not long after I had come to Aunt Barbara's home, Opa and Oma Hoeger come to visit and bring my little sister, Erna.

"We have brought Erna so that she and Kaethi can be together," they tell Baewibas. "We hope she can stay with you. We have little room at our daughter's house for Erna."

My aunt and uncle Findeis agree and we make room for another bed on the floor. I am happy to have Erna with me, but feel sad that my father's sister could not help out with our care.

Now there is another mouth to feed, but it's nice to have Erna with me. She is four years old and doesn't really understand why she is being shuffled around. At least I can look after her while the adults have to work for the partisans during the day. She often asks for Mami and it's hard for me to tell her the truth.

War on Orphans, Illness and Death

G akowa is now known as one of the many death camps. There are others in Rudolfsgnad, Jarek, Mitrovica and Kruschiwl. The children in the camp without parents must face the new ordinance to be shipped out to an orphanage in a Communist oriented upbringing.

One of the favorite pastimes of the partisans is to have us assemble in the empty field at the north end of town near St. Anthony's Chapel. There, they line us up and pick out the able-bodied men and boys for work, or their choice of the women for their pleasure.

One day, we hear that all children, whose parents are dead or in other labor camps or prison camps, are to be brought to the town hall to be taken to an orphanage in the south of Yugoslavia. They are to be educated in the Communist idealism and raised as future soldiers for Tito. The children will never see their parents or relatives again. Even if the parents should return from labor camps or war camps, they will never find them and the children will never know that they are of German heritage.

My aunt and Altmutter decide that my sister Erna and I will be hidden for a period of time to escape this cruel punishment. Where to go? There is no time to lose!

Altmutter takes Erna, myself and the daughter of my godmother, Katharina Rettig, whose mother was taken to Russia and whose father is a prisoner of war, and hides us in the attic of her sister's house. The partisans search each house for the children because they know that some are in hiding. We are afraid they will find us there, so we are moved to another part of the house. There we climb into an ice storage container. Altmutter's sister has a Wirtshaus, just like my parents. The ice storage container had been used to cool the beer and wine at one time. Now it is empty. It is large enough for us three children, but it is hard to keep us quiet. I am the oldest and try to keep the two smaller children amused and calm their fears. It is dark and cold in our hiding place, but Altmutter brings warm clothes and some food and water.

"Children, you must be quiet," cautions Altmutter. "The partisans are searching this whole block."

"I will tell them some stories, Altmutter, and keep them amused," I whisper.

The four and seven year olds are not easy to keep quiet in a small dark space. They wiggle and fidget as most children will do. I have a piece of string and teach them how to play "cat in a cradle." That is a quiet game which makes them think a little.

We hold our breath when we hear the harsh voices of the partisans in the house. They bellow their commands and we hear their footsteps coming closer. They open the doors to all the rooms, the cellar and the attic. I am sure Altmutter's heart must have stopped for a moment when they approached our hiding place.

Our Guardian Angel must have been very close! We are not found during our three day stay in hiding. Finally, we hear that the collected children are being shipped out and we are free to come out of hiding. When we return to my aunt's house, she is happy to see us and glad we had not been found.

"Just say you are my daughter, in case anyone asks you," she tells me.

"There are always people who will report you in order to get favors from the partisans. It is sad that your own people will go against you."

"Yes, Baewibas, I will remember."

———————————— ✳ ————————————

Each day there is some punishment being dealt out. A drunken partisan searches the house of my godmother, Katharina Rettig. She has been taken to a Russian labor camp, but her seven year old daughter, Katharina Jr. lives there with her grandmother, Maria Rettig. The partisan finds an empty bicycle tool bag and takes it to be a handgun holster. He pins her to a wall; his rifle pointed ready to shoot. This is taking place while the seven year old Katharina and the great-grandmother have to watch. Another partisan stopped the shooting, but feels this cannot go unpunished. So they bind Maria's hands behind her back with a wire. They throw her down the ten step cellar stairs and pull her back up by her hair. They repeat this over and over, while Maria's cries reach all over the house.

Little Katharina runs to call Maria's daughter and son-in-law, who live a few blocks away, and they explain to the partisans that the item they found is only a bicycle tool bag and plead for them to stop. This seems to have satisfied the partisans and they finally release Maria. She is taken to her daughter's house. They care for her bleeding hands, cut almost to the bone from the wire. Her face is bruised and her whole body is black and blue. She is not able to lift her arms and needs care for a long time. Maria never returns to her home again and little Katharina is taken to her maternal grandparents, Anton and Barbara Findeis. She will live there with my sister Erna and Altmutter.

———————————— ✳ ————————————

The food which is distributed to each person is cooked in a large kettle in certain homes on each street. Corn bread without salt accompanies the soup. The watered-down soup has little nourishment. Peas or beans sparsely float on top; the only meat might be some flies or bugs that landed in it. The people have to walk and get their allotted food in their own container. The corn bread is often hard as a rock. The sick, who cannot get up to pick up their food, often go hungry.

The summer of 1945 has brought much sickness—typhoid fever rages on and now malaria is taking over. Fifty to sixty people die each day. Lice and insects and rodents carry the disease from one person to another. Burial becomes a problem. A large hole is dug behind our regular cemetery. The bodies are wrapped in a cloth and buried in rows stacked up to the top. No markers, no coffins, no dignity!

Each day the *Totenwagen* (death wagon) drives up and down the streets, collecting the bodies left outside each house. It is a horse-less wagon pulled by camp inhabitants who are assigned to this heartless task. The relatives may not accompany their loved ones to the cemetery. The corpses are stacked on top of each other in the wagon, sometimes their arms dangling from the side of the wagon, and taken to the cemetery where they are buried in mass graves.

The relatives of the dead pin their name and place of birth to the corpse. At the cemetery, one man is in charge of keeping track of how many corpses are brought to the cemetery each day. The men and women, whose task it is to bury the corpses, often faint from the stench of the bodies in the heat of the summer.

More and more people are brought to camp. The incoming victims take the place of those who died. Those who are still able to work are taken out each morning to work in the fields, tending the corn and beans grown for the camp's food. Some of the men must pull wagons out into the surrounding fields to collect firewood.

Some of the women, who work in the fields, are so weak from hunger that they pass out. Others must do double work to make up for them. When it pleases the partisans, they line up the women and inspect them. Their eyes gleaming with lust, they walk up and down, taunting and shouting obscenities.

"I will come with you," a voice is heard, as one of the women steps out of line.

The other women are shocked and want to pull her back. She whispers to them:

"I will sacrifice myself for all of you."

The partisan stands in front of her in disbelief as she looks him straight in the eye.

He walks away, perhaps not finding any pleasure without force. And so another day ends without any consequences, thanks to this brave lady. Aunt Barbara tells us of this incident when she arrives home that evening.

As fall approaches, it is harder and harder to find anything to burn. Will there be enough firewood for the coming winter months? Fences, barns and trees are being cut down.

I have outgrown my one pair of leather shoes and must now wear woolen slippers which my grandmother made for me. My cousin, who is two years older than I, has outgrown her shoes, so I will have a pair for the winter. We try to find a pair of shoes for Erna, too, and are able to bargain with a family in exchange for some food.

It is getting close to Christmas, 1945. Erna and I look forward to the holiday, because it is a special day. Remembering the wonderful holidays we spent with our family, we feel the loneliness of this first Christmas without our parents. We hope that our father is alive and will come for us.

On Christmas Eve, after our meager meal of corn bread and soup, we decorate a barren tree limb with some cloth remnants given to us by the seamstress and sing Christmas songs.

Stille Nacht, Heilige Nacht, the familiar Christmas song is sung with special reverence. As we look out, snow is softly falling from the sky, as if to bring us blessings from above. It is a melancholy night as we all sing and then tell stories of the good times. Each person tells of a special Christmas they had experienced. We fall asleep in peace that night.

A few days after Christmas, Altvater Nikolaus comes down with typhoid fever. He is very ill, the fever is high. Altmutter already knows about this disease because she cared for my mother and me. She is again the caregiver, the stronger one! I am not allowed to visit because I might have a relapse of the disease. We are all very concerned about him and have little hope of his recovery.

On January 6, 1946, he takes his last breath. We are allowed to bury him in the same grave with my mother. Now we have lost three close family members since the concentration camp began—my mother, Altvater and his mother who died in Kruschiwl in 1944.

Altmutter's house is filled with people from other towns, but she feels lonesome. She has lost two of the most important people in her life—her husband and her daughter.

"Kaethi, can you come and stay with me for awhile so I am not so alone," she asks me.

I move again taking my few belongings with me. Among the pieces of clothing, I have hidden my favorite toy made out of a corn husk. It is a corn husk doll. The husk is the coat and the corn silk resembles the hair. I braid the hair while I pretend she is a beautiful doll made out of porcelain. Erna stays with the Findeis family.

The Flotz Family Journey Continues

*I*t is August, 1945. Anna Flotz and her three boys have been drift-
*ing around Europe on trains, transported from one place to an-
other. They are now in Bacsalmas in Hungary in a train that has
been stopped on a side track, waiting for another train to pass.*

While the train was parked on a side-track, we boys found water
so my mother could wash our clothes. It was a hot August day and
the clothes would dry fast. Suddenly, we heard the whistle of an oncoming train, which passed slowly through the station. The sign at
the train station read: Bacsalmas.

"Look out boys and stay away from the tracks," Mom called out
to us.

She had a pail of water and was ready to toss it out the door of
the train, when the oncoming train slowly passed. As she looked
out, she screamed: "Oh my God, it's George. It's my husband."

The men in the passing train all looked out to see a man jump
off. It was my father! The men threw his belongings out the door
and cheered at this miraculous reunion. My mother, brothers and I
jumped off our train and ran to meet him. Hugs and kisses, crying
and laughing, all melting into one wonderful moment.

I could not believe this was my father. A man of 42, who looked
like 60, stood before us. He was unshaven, his hair hidden under a
tattered hat, his clothes dirty and mismatched and his shoes scuffed
and torn. In just ten months, he had aged and his appearance

changed dramatically. But, we must have looked the same to him. Some of our clothes were too small, some too large. We were thin and undernourished, and weary from our journey. What the hardships of war can do to a family.

"Where have you been and where are you going?" asked my father. "Let's get your things and we'll go into town." We all talked at once and we could not believe what surely must be a miracle.

"George, we have been wandering around Europe since last October, trying to evade the Russians. We were on our way home to Bezdan, when we were told that the German people are in concentration camps," my mother explains.

Before we left the train, we said goodbye to the Glass family, Aunt Theresa, Anna and Karl. They were going to continue on the train towards Austria.

"Where are *you* coming from?" we asked.

"It's a long story and I will tell you all about it once we find a place to stay. Now let's get your things, boys, and help your mother," said my father. We grabbed our bundles and walked into town.

The first place we stopped was at a blacksmith's shop and my father asked for work. There was no job for him. However, we continued on and finally we found a blacksmith who needed help.

We were overjoyed that he found work. The only pay he received was his meals and lodging for us in one room located in the back of the blacksmith's house. My mother found housework in exchange for her meals and was able to take little Johnnie along. Lorenz and I hired out as laborers on the surrounding farms for our food.

We were content to stay here because this town was only 50 kilometers from Bezdan, our hometown. We still had hopes of being able to return one day, after the border between Hungary and Yugoslavia opened up and the people in the concentration camps were freed.

This would never happen.

————————— ✳ —————————

One evening, while we all sat together, my father told us the story of how he came to travel this way. During his days in the German army, he never received a uniform or a gun. He was assigned to work as a blacksmith, his trade. The horses used in the war needed to be shod and he was kept out of the active fighting. Later, during the chaos of the final days, he deserted, taking a wagon and horses with him. He had hoped to make it back home.

However, he was caught by the Russians while traveling through Czechoslovakia. They took away the horses and wagon and most of his possessions. He was taken to Auschwitz Concentration Camp, famous for the Jewish extermination. This camp, located in Poland, was now used for POWs.

In the camp, my father was able to find some ether, build a still and brew alcohol. He traded the alcohol for cigarettes from the guards and then traded the cigarettes for food from the POWs. Since he was not in uniform nor armed, he was considered harmless and was soon released after a few months. He was put on a train from Poland to Yugoslavia and on this incredible journey, our paths crossed.

We then took turns telling our father about our journey into the various countries and the dangers we encountered. He could not believe how my mother managed to survive with us three boys while traveling all over Europe. She was certainly not afraid of anything and fought her way through many crises. Her small stature did not stop her.

My mother met a German lady from Baja, a town 15 kilometers away, who was looking for a boy to help out on their farm.

"Would you like to come and work for us?" she asked me. "Our son is a prisoner of war and we need someone to replace him on our farm."

I was only 13 years old but it would help my family with one less mouth to feed. I hated to leave my family, but reluctantly I did.

"Will you be all right, George?" my mother worried. "I hate to see you be alone in Baja."

I did not let her see my tears; I did not tell her about my fears to be all alone with strangers because I knew it would help the family. I packed up my things, said goodbye to everyone and went with the lady.

The first morning, at breakfast, two bowls of milk and some bread were on the table. I was very hungry and started to eat, and before I knew it, I had finished all the milk and bread. When the farmer came in from the field, he found me at the table, but there was no food for him. He was not angry; he just smiled at me, as if to say that he understood. The next morning, however, I found only one bowl of milk.

My job was to herd the cows in the meadow. This was a great opportunity for me to get as much milk as I liked. I knew how to milk a cow, so I merely aimed the udder in my direction. Then, I looked for vegetables in the fields, especially potatoes, or I picked fruit from the trees along the highway. Thank God for those fruit trees along the highways!

On Sundays I was free to go home, if I liked. I walked the 15 kilometers because I was homesick and there was no other way to get there. Then, I walked back later in the day, happy to have seen my family.

In the spring of 1946, my employers, who were also ethnic Germans, were stripped of their land and possessions by the Communists. They left the country, just as we had done, and I returned to my family in Bacsalmas.

Gakowa—1946

Gakowa has become a place for the living dead. Illness and starvation is the daily topic of discussion. The winter is harsh and the partisans even harsher. Plans are being made to segregate the sick from the others in the camp.

I am now living with Altmutter in her home on the north end of town. She had barely gotten over my mother's death, when Altvater succumbed to typhoid fever. It is a terrible time for her.

One day, soon after I moved in with her, we see partisans coming into the yard, shouting for us to pack up and leave. A translator tells us that this part of town will be the new hospital for all the sick, a make-shift "leper colony." This will contain the typhoid and malaria and keep it from spreading. We must leave in 15 minutes.

Altmutter packs a few things and dresses me in layers of clothes to keep warm. We leave the house to go back to Aunt Barbara, and in our haste, we forget to take my only pair of shoes. I had been wearing my woolen slippers in the house. We ask permission to go back for the shoes, but the partisans push us to leave and refuse to let us go back. I am crying but Altmutter pulls me along so that no further attention is called to us. She does not want any problems with the partisans.

The few things that we own, Altvater's clothes and some household articles we could have used to barter for food, are left for the partisans to take.

I am heartbroken because the few personal things I had saved, some from my mother, are now gone. Altmutter and I walk briskly to get out of the cold. With heavy bundles and a heavy heart we arrive at Aunt Barbara's house. My sister is happy to see me and I, too, had missed her. Room is made on the floor for our stay.

About a month later, rumors circulate that the partisans will segregate the children of the camp into one area. The small children, whose mothers were spared the trip to Russia and other work camps, are now to be separated so that the mothers can work in the camp in Gakowa. They must do labor in the surrounding fields, work for the partisans as house-keepers or tend to the sick.

The day arrives when the town crier announces the movement of the children. We are to pack our things and wait in our houses for the partisans to come and pick us up. Erna and I have been prepared for the move:

"Just stay close together and you'll be all right," councils Altmutter. "Maybe this will not last too long and you will be back."

"I don't want to go," cries Erna. "I want to stay here."

What will happen to us without adult supervision? I fear the abuse and mistreatment of the partisans. They are known for their cruelty to adults, why not the children? I am scared!

We sit and wait. Time passes slowly. It is also one of the coldest days this winter. It is just another way to punish and torture us. It has started to snow and the clouds darken the skies earlier than usual. I am in my woolen slippers. If I have to go out in this weather, the snow will soon penetrate my slippers and freeze my toes.

No one comes to get us on this day! We hear from the neighbors that this movement has been cancelled. Is it because this is too much trouble for the partisans, or are they too cold to carry out this order? Everyone is ordered to return to their families. What stupidity, what unnecessary hardship, what cruelty to the children. Thank God it is over.

With the tension gone, we can sleep soundly again. At least until the next time.

We have, however, another problem causing me sleepless nights. It is the presence of large numbers of rodents that are over-running the camp.

I am deathly afraid of mice and rats. I wonder what they eat. There is little enough food for the people, let alone these rodents, but these creatures seem to thrive and multiply in the camp. They live in the walls of the house, scratch and scrape until they can find a hole to come out and run around during the night. I suppose they also wish to survive, as we do, but they cannot be tolerated. Altmutter's job each morning is to plaster up the holes in the walls. How I dread going to sleep each night, knowing that they will run and crawl over us. Sometimes we find them in our shoes in the morning.

This fear will be my lifelong phobia.

A New Home
for Me

My mother's brother and sister in law, Michael and Justina Brandt, will become a part of my life for now and in the future.

My mother's brother, Michael Brandt, was not drafted into the German army in 1944 due to health problems. He was not taken to the Russian Labor Camps because he spoke the Serbian language and the partisans needed some people to be interpreters in the camp. But in the spring of 1946, he is called to a work detail in the town of Kernei, in the brick factory.

After he leaves, my aunt Justina comes to ask me to stay with her. Their house has been filled with the furniture from the other houses in Gakowa, but she is allowed one room to live in. Another family from Sentiwan, Katie Scheschowitsch and her daughter Resi and son Tony, live in one of the other empty rooms and they are responsible for milking all the cows in the barn. Aunt Justina is lucky to work in a bakery that also bakes bread for the partisans—white bread. She always hides a few pieces of bread in her clothing each day for us to eat. Sometimes she is able to steal a little flour, so we are lucky to have more food.

One day, a partisan comes to the house. It is a day when aunt Justina is not working. He tells her to come into the yard and when she does, he points the rifle at her and starts to scream in Serbian. She does not understand him but wonders what he wants of her.

My uncle is away in Kernei at this time, so she cannot get help from him. Finally, another partisan comes into the yard and pulls him away, grabbing the rifle from him. He explains that this is the wife of their interpreter and to leave her alone.

He pushes his comrade forward and out of the house. My aunt stumbles into the house and breaks down crying. I find her like this when I come home from playing with some friends down the street.

"What happened, Justinabas?" I ask her, bringing her some water to drink.

"Oh, child, I am lucky to be alive," she begins and then tells me the whole story.

She is shaking all over her body, spilling some of the water she is trying to drink. I comfort her and listen as she describes what happened. I am glad I did not have to see it because it would have frightened me to death. How long can we endure the abuse and torture of these uncontrolled guardians of this camp? Justinabas and I cry together and I hold her while she sobs. We sit like this until the sun begins to set and we close the curtains and lock the door. Neither one of us is hungry that day.

It is another day of assembly at the St. Anthony's Chapel grounds. What will the commandant do today? There are not too many able bodied men and women left in Gakowa. Will they now take the old people to labor camps?

My aunt is frightened. Although she works in the bakery, they might pick her out for hard labor somewhere in another town. My uncle, who might have been able to save her because of his language skills, is not here now. She has a key to all the rooms and decides not to go to the assembly but hide in one of the rooms that are filled with the furniture. The furniture has been stored over a year. It is dusty and houses spiders, bugs and, probably, rodents.

"I am afraid to go into this room!" I cry. "There may be rats and spiders crawling around." My aunt is sympathetic, but firm: I must go with her. I am shaking with fear that the soldiers will find us in there anyway. The Scheschowitsch family staying in our house also hides with my aunt and me. The adults hide behind large pieces of furniture and the children crawl into the standing dressers with doors. We must be very quiet because the partisans go from house to house and look for those that fail to come to assembly. They carry their guns, ready to shoot.

All of a sudden, we hear the footsteps of the partisans. We hear them shout, "Come out or we will shoot!" They open doors to the rooms, barns and cellar, but my aunt has locked the door to the room in which we are hiding. They look in the windows, but we are well hidden. I am so frightened that I feel the urge to go to the bathroom. I cannot move, so I do the inevitable. If we are caught, it might cost us our lives. The partisans' anger is acted out viciously when their orders are not obeyed. They think nothing of shooting down anyone at the slightest excuse.

After some terrifying moments, they finally leave the house. When we hear people returning from assembly, we, too, come out of hiding, relieved and thankful.

The time passes slowly for the children. There is no schooling and we are bored. This is the time for learning, but we sit idle. One day, a lady comes to visit and asks if I would like to come to religious education to prepare for my First Holy Communion. The priests in town, Father Wendelin Gruber and Father Mathias Johler, are giving secret classes in various places where they are not noticed by the partisans. I am glad to go—anxious to learn, and I am glad to be with other children. We learn the basics for receiving Communion; the Ten Commandments, preparation for going to Confession, the various prayers of the Catholic Church, and some Bible stories. It is hard to comprehend the lessons of right and wrong when you see the daily torture, the inhuman treatment of people, the sickness and hunger without receiving help. The priest says we are in the hands of God and He will give us strength. Our church is still open although the partisans frown upon Masses being held. However, plans are being made for May 19, 1946. That will be the day that 600 children will receive Holy Communion. We are told to wear clean clothes and if we can find some wild flowers, to make a wreath for our heads. The wreaths should be put on after we get inside the church.

Father Gruber has made arrangements with a kind baker in the town of Sombor to provide some baked goods for the children on this special day. Father Gruber is still "free" and not considered a camp inhabitant. He may leave the town whenever he wishes. I guess it is the respect for the priesthood that the commandant has allowed this privilege. But for how long?

I feel special this day, and think of how proud my mother would be of me. Surely, she is watching me from above. My mother had a great devotion to the Blessed Mother. She taught me to say the rosary and often prayed with me. After my father left for the army, we prayed each night for him.

"If your father returns to us, safe and sound," she would tell me, "we will have a statue of the Blessed Mother erected in the church in thanksgiving."

It is a beautiful, sunny day. The rays of the sun stream into the church through the stained-glass windows. Some of the pews are filled with relatives and the rest are reserved for all the children. Father Mathias Johler, and Father Wendelin Gruber, the attending priests, stand at the foot of the altar as we all march down the isle to our designated pew. They are smiling to reassure us. What if the soldiers come in and stop us? They can do anything they want to. They have the guns. We are excited but a little afraid.

But we are lucky and the Mass continues. We each walk up to the altar to receive the Holy Communion, all of us hoping that this blessing will keep us safe.

"Dear children, today is a very important day in your life. You will carry this with you throughout your life. Be strong and have faith, and God will stand by you," the priest tells us. He is a kind man, and we loved learning from him. His smile comforts us. I will never forget this day. A Holy Card with the inscription of the occasion and the date is given to each of us. This keepsake I will keep all my life.

My relatives have come to church and brought me a bunch of wild flowers. There is no white dress or a veil. A simple, clean garment would have to do.

Before the partisans realize what we are doing, the ceremony is over. We quietly file out of church, content in the realization that we have "put one over on them." We march into the rectory's garden and await our treats. We have just received the Body of Christ in the form of Communion and now we are given *Kipfel*—a type of croissant. What joy in this simple pleasure!

In the summer of 1946, my uncle Michael returns from Kernei. Now, I am less afraid because he is here with us.

The summer months are hot. The only water comes from the well in the yard. We use it for drinking and to wash our clothes and

Andenken
an meine
Erstkommunion
im Lager
zu Gakowa
19. II. 1946.

I made my First Communion in the Lager Gakowa, May 19, 1946.

our bodies. Some of the wells in town have run dry because of all the people using water. When it rains, we save the water. The grass and any vegetables growing in the small garden must wait for God's blessing from above—a cool rain.

On hot evenings, the young people gather outside the home of the local bandleader, which is across the street from our house. His son, Hans Kern, sits outside and plays his accordion. He plays the well known folk songs about hearth and home, about returning soldiers from the war, about better times in the future. I have always loved music. Tobias used to take accordion lessons with a group of his friends at Mr. Kern's house in previous years, and I would always go with him, when I visited, just to hear the class practice. So, I am now in the group listening and singing along. The music gives people hope and lifts their spirits in this dismal place and these trying times. It is an outlet for their breaking hearts and brings them relief from the daily horrors of the camp.

It is a mystery to me why the partisans allow us to gather and sing. I wonder if they also enjoy a few moments of peace in this unbearable place. In fact, sometimes they ask Hans to play some Serbian songs and they, too, sing along.

One day I notice some boils on my hands, especially between my fingers. They are painful and filled with pus. There is also one on my shoulder. We cannot determine what causes these boils—perhaps the lack of proper nutrition or proper cleanliness. We have no more soap to clean ourselves, just water. Some of the women suggest that I wash the boils in my own urine while it is still warm.

"I don't want to put my hands in the urine," I object. "It is disgusting."

"Please, Kaethi, let's try it," my aunt pleads, "We must do something."

I finally give in and find out that it does help. The boils open up, the pus comes out and the wound dries up. We depend a great deal on home remedies.

We see the death rate grow each day by the many trips the Totenwagen must make to collect the corpses. My aunt and uncle discuss our situation:

"Should we try to escape?" my aunt wonders. "We can't stay here much longer."

The neighbors often discuss this amongst themselves, but they always hope that this will end soon. We are still in our own town, in our houses, but how long can we survive?

"There is talk that soon the camp will be dissolved," one of the neighbors, Frau Puhler tells us.

"I think that is just a lot of propaganda," my uncle Michael replies. "The commandant just wants to improve the morale among the *Lagersleut*—the camp inhabitants."

There are more assemblies; we stand in the hot sun, the men lined up at one end and the women and children at the other. The commandant followed by the gun-toting partisans marches up and down, looking over his prisoners. He picks and chooses at his discretion—one man for labor, another for punishment; one woman for camp duty, another for his pleasure. We children are not too patient, but if we don't stand still, the adults will be punished. I am old enough to understand, but the little toddlers are hard to control.

How will all this end?

Escape—Flight on
the Wings of Fear

Preparations *are made for our escape from the concentration
camp in August 1947.*
    The decision to escape the camp and leave family,
neighbors, home, and town is a big one for my aunt and uncle.
What if they leave, and their son Tobias is released from the Russian
labor camp and comes back home? They will not be here. I am also
distressed to think that it will be almost impossible to find my father
again. I worry about when I would see my sister, Erna, again. She
will stay with the Findeis family and Altmutter in the camp.

One of Tobias' close friends, who also left on that train to Russia
in December 1944, was able to escape from there and return home
to Gakowa. He told us all about the life the prisoners endured in
Russia. He told us about Tobias—what he endured and how they
all managed to survive. It was devastating for my aunt and uncle
to hear about this. Perhaps Tobias would not be able to survive the
hardships; he is only 20 and has been in Russia for three years. We
hear that some of the sick and disabled prisoners have been released
into Germany from Russia because they no longer were of any use
to the Communists. Maybe he is among them and we can find him
there.

Then there is the separation from my sister, if they take me with
them on their journey to Germany. At the age of 12, I can feel the
disappointment and sorrow of leaving my 6 year old sister. But, I

must accept whatever my relatives decide.

"You will see Erna again," Justinabas tells me. "One day we will all go to America."

My aunt's parents, Frank and Theresia Dsida, had immigrated to America in the 1920's and will surely help us once we get to Germany. My aunt's father had just died in 1946, but her mother may be able to send us food once we get out of here.

It is decided! We will leave in late August 1947. We prepare the few things we can carry but must keep quiet about our plans so as not to be reported. The farewells are hard. Tears and hugs and a few words of encouragement are all I can leave my sister. She cries and clings to me, as I do to her. But she is accustomed, as am I, to do what we are told. I also take leave from our father's parents, Opa and Oma Hoeger, who will stay in Gakowa. Our family has taken on a big burden to help us—it is twice as hard because of the danger involved. We are grateful!

Our destination is Ludwigsburg, Germany, where a relative of my aunt lives. However, if my aunt and uncle Findeis were to leave the camp with my sister, they would have no special place to go. They will have to notify us in Ludwigsburg, and tell us of their whereabouts.

---------------------------- ✳ ----------------------------

It is a cool night in August. The town of Gakowa is enveloped in darkness and the streets are quiet. Each night some of the inhabitants of the camp try to escape from this hamlet of hell by walking about five kilometers to the Hungarian border and crossing to freedom. Tonight, we are among them.

We sit on our bundles near the edge of town, waiting for our guide to tell us when to go. He waits for the changing of the guards, and while waiting, we must be very quiet. The tension heightens as the hours pass. I am afraid of the dark, of all the things I cannot see and especially of the partisans that stand guard around the town. Finally, it is time! We pick up our bundles and begin walking in line. I am being pushed along by the adults because I cannot walk as fast. My bundle is heavy and my legs are short—I am only 12.

To avoid being seen, we travel mostly through corn fields. The corn stalks hit me in the face as I walk. I am scared of what may be on the ground, snakes, mice and other things which frighten a child. But, there is no time to worry about that now—just keep moving.

It is so dark and I am so tired! Will I be able to make it all the way? The weight of my bundle is pushing me down, and the layers of clothes which I am wearing, to avoid carrying them, is making me very hot. It is important that I keep my clothes on because all the valuables we have are sewn into the linings of my garments.

There is whispering among the adults. "Are we going the right way? Are we close?"

All of a sudden, our guide gives us the signal that we are approaching the border. Everyone is quiet, holding their breath for a safe crossing. Then, there is a sudden loud cry:

"Stoj!" a well known command in the camp, tells us we must stop.

Our guide has vanished. He has returned to the camp in order to bring more people across the border the next night. We realize the horrible fact that we have been captured. The soldiers come running out of the border station and surround us, shouting words I cannot understand, but I know they are bad news for us.

Normally, when captured, the group is returned to the camp and imprisoned for a few days in the cellar of a house, with no light, no food, no water and no toilet facilities. Often they are tortured and left to die. This was to "teach us a lesson."

I start to cry and shake with fear. My aunt and uncle hold and comfort me, but they, too, fear the worst.

"What will they do to us?" I cry and imagine the long walk back. "I am so tired and cannot walk anymore."

We are told to walk to the border station and sit down. We do so gladly as long as we do not have to return to the camp. By this time, dawn creeps slowly in and the sun rises to another hot August day. We are not alone; at the border station there are other groups who have been captured that night.

As the day progresses, each family is interrogated and searched. Any valuables they find will become the property of the guards. They pay little attention to the children, so I am safe. Finally, after everyone is searched, the Commandant of the station starts to preach to us.

"I will let you go, but you must promise to stay in the Russian Zone and you will be treated well by the Communists."

We cannot believe our good luck, and we assure him that we will do what he says. My uncle, who understands Serbian tells the others what the Commandant has said. The people are relieved and express thanks to him for letting us go on to Hungary. Even though we are still under Communist-occupied Hungary, we are no longer imprisoned and are able to move freely.

"Why is he letting us go?" the people around us comment. "Maybe this man has a heart and our prayers have been answered," my uncle replies. This seems like a miracle to me. Are they finally letting us go to empty the camp so that they are rid of us? I feel like there is someone looking out for me. Could it be my mother?

I am exhausted and fall asleep in the yard. As evening approaches, my aunt wakes me to continue our journey. Unbelievable as it seems, we are free to cross the border into Hungary. The first hurdle of our long journey has been accomplished and we walk towards our expected goal—freedom.

CHAPTER
ELEVEN

A Step at a Time,
A Day at a Time

A fter our release from the border guards, our group from the concentration camp "Gakowa" decides to spread out and go towards Hungary in smaller groups.

There are nine in our group. My aunt, uncle and I, my grandfather's brother Stefan Brandt and his wife, Appolonia, Stefan and Barbara Hirn, and Theresia Sehn and her granddaughter, Julia. It is a coincidence that all of us have relatives in America. Some have parents, others have children there. We are all from Gakowa and we stay together for the entire trip.

Julia, who is about my age, also lost her mother to typhoid fever in the camp. Her father is in the German army. We both hope to find our fathers in Germany. Julia and I have become friends.

"What are you going to do when you get to Germany?" asks Julia. "Are you looking forward to going to school?"

"I am afraid we are going to be dumb compared to the other children," I reply anxiously. "I hope to find an understanding teacher."

Julia and I have many such questions. We spend all our time together while the adults look for food and transportation. We try to find ways to pass the time by playing word games, drawing in the sand with sticks, collecting pretty flowers or leaves. We admire the new surroundings we see each day.

The first night of our new-found freedom we spend in a farmer's barn. The hay is softer than the ground we slept on the night before and the farmer lets us wash at his well in the morning. He gives us a little milk and bread, and after my uncle and the other men bargain with him, he agrees to provide us with transportation in his wagon. The older people are able to ride in the wagon with the baggage while the young ones walk. After a day's journey, he drops us off at a small town, where we can register and get further instructions for travel.

The men in the group always have to find ways to move along the countryside, staying away from any place where soldiers can question us. We are free from a concentration camp, but still under suspicion. We have no papers or passports, and are called *Fluechtlinge*—displaced persons. The country is occupied and controlled by Russian soldiers and the ruling government is now Communist.

After traveling a few days, we have become quite dirty. But, except for the great outdoors, we have no toilet facilities. Other than a small stream or a generous farmer's well, there is no place to wash our clothes or ourselves. Our food is running out. We try to pick the fruit off the trees along the highways or find potatoes in the fields already harvested. My uncle makes a small fire by the side of the road. We cut up the potatoes and cook them in our dented and soot-covered pot until they are crisp and golden brown.

"Would you like some potatoes?" my aunt asks, passing the pot.

I smack my lips and rub my stomach, reaching for a helping. "I love potatoes, and these taste wonderful," I compliment my aunt. We finish off every bite and hope that we find some more food the next day.

Many refugees are on the roads and in the various refugee camps along the way. The Russians know we are here and try to move us along to another country. In one of the camps, we find out that some trucks will take us close to the Austrian border. We are happy to pack up and go again.

"Kaethi, come and get your *Rucksack* (backpack) so we can get on the truck," my aunt calls to me.

"Come, Julia," I call to my friend, "I guess we're getting a ride today."

Many other refugees get on the trucks and we are crowded together, holding on to each other so as not to fall down. The truck is old and the road is bumpy. It is pretty hot, but I have never been on a big truck, so it's a real adventure for me. Soon, someone starts to sing, and more and more people join in.

> *Heimatlos sind viele auf der Welt*
> Homeless are many in this world
> *Heimatlos und einsam bin ich*
> Homeless and lonely am I
> *Ueberall verdiene ich mein Geld*
> In many places I earn my daily bread
> *Doch keiner wartet auf mich*
> Yet no one waits for me

The sad strains of the song build into a crescendo of tears.

We arrive at a railroad station and board a train which takes us close to the Austrian border. We have no money, but all refugees are allowed on the trains free.

Soon we must leave the train again because, without a passport, we cannot cross into Austria. The train stops at a town in which a refugee camp is set up. We are again taken into a room, searched for valuables or money and then released.

Horse-drawn wagons are waiting to take us to the Austrian border. Only the old and the children can ride; the rest must walk. It is raining; the water-soaked dirt road makes the journey even harder. The day begins to turn dark earlier than usual and the walking is treacherous when you cannot see.

When we arrive at the border, we are pleased to see the Austrian border patrol waiting for us with trucks. Thank God, we can all ride again and don't have to carry our bundles. However, we are still in the Russian Zone and must find a way to cross over into the American Zone.

※

Austria is a very beautiful country and very different from our home. There are majestic mountains, pine forests, meadows dotted with black and white cows grazing in the sunshine. I have never seen anything like it. I marvel at the ever-changing landscapes, the peaceful small towns bustling with refugees looking for a place to sleep, some food or even a temporary job in exchange for their livelihood.

We are trying to get into the American Zone in Austria. Our group collects their valuables so we can try and hire a truck to take us near the border. We will need to find a guide to help us cross over the difficult border station when we get close enough to begin walking.

"I will take you to Vienna," the truck driver tells us. "You can then find other means of travel from there. I cannot go further than that."

We are grateful and get ready to move on.

"I heard that Vienna is beautiful and is the City of Music," my uncle comments, "but it may be difficult to move about because the city is divided into four zones, American, Russian, English and French."

Julia and I are excited to see our first big city. However, when we arrive, there is devastation all around. Buildings are bombed out, the Opera House is severely damaged, and there is rubble and dirt everywhere. The supplies are rationed because of the great number of people entering the country. Food and clothing, as well as housing, are scarce.

You must be a resident to get ration cards, so we are unable to get anything. We must beg or try to barter our belongings for food.

We take public transportation to the outskirts of Vienna. While on the bus, we encounter some Russian soldiers. Our appearance and the baggage we carry identify us clearly as refugees.

I whisper to my aunt, "Are they going to arrest us?"

"Look, they are leaving the bus," she whispers back. "This time we are in luck."

After leaving the bus, we see an old shack where we can take shelter for the night. Again we settle down, trying to rest while the men decide how to proceed.

"Let's take turns waving down vehicles for a ride," my uncle suggests to the other men in the group. They agree and station themselves near the road. Just before dawn, we find a kindly person who will take us closer to the border.

We leave the truck again and begin walking into the pine forest in the direction that the driver gave us. He has instructed us where to find a guide to help us make our way across the border. It is drizzling again and the pine needles stick to our shoes. The baggage also gets wet.

"My feet are so cold and wet," I complain.

"Let's see, Kaethi, maybe we can wrap something around your feet," my aunt suggests.

She tears up a pillow case and wraps it around my feet. This helps keep me warm. I am amazed that we have not caught a cold or flu. We must be in the hands of God. My uncle has stomach problems, and many times he is in pain. We don't know what is causing it, but suspect an ulcer. But he is able to keep going.

As we wait for darkness to come, our only companion is the rain, a friend who stays by our side. In bad weather, there is less chance of being detected. We have our guide with us who leads us along the paths in the forest.

We finally leave the forest and approach an area with many hills. We climb up the slippery wet grass-covered hill and then get the signal to retreat because of approaching guards. We slide down the hill quickly, taking the shrubs and mud with us. We must repeat this several times but have no luck in crossing the border.

"We must take the most dangerous path," the guide whispers. "It is the only way to get across before daylight."

We are tired and worn out, but determined and we begin again to climb the designated hill. Our efforts are hampered by the wet grass. We climb up a few feet and slide down again.

"I can't go any further!" I cry. "Please help me."

I have a pebble in my shoe that really hurts me.

My uncle comes behind me and pushes me up, meanwhile holding on to anything that he can grab to steady himself. We hear voices from the top.

"Oh no, there is barbed wire at the top of the hill. How will we get across?"

The guide quickly cuts some of the wire and several people help pull the wires apart to let us pass through. I cut my hand and some of my clothes get caught. The hem of my dress is torn.

"Don't worry about your dress, Kaethi, just hurry up and push your bag through the hole," I am instructed. I am finally on the other side, relieved and exhausted.

There is a road that we need to cross for the final step into the American Zone. However, a mill with a flood light rotating on top of its building lights up the road every minute. In the moments when the road is dark, our guide quickly pushes us across. One by one, we take the final steps to the other side.

The guide takes us to a nearby farm house, where we can stay for the night in the farmer's barn. Will we ever sleep in a bed again?

We have conquered another mission in our flight. We now need to cross into Germany.

One More Border to Cross, Austria to Germany

*O*ur journey is getting us closer to our destination. We are tired, dirty and long for a good night's sleep in a bed.
The following morning we are awakened by our natural alarm clock—the sun. It is time to move on. We pick up our belongings, sling them on our backs and begin another journey towards our final destination. The other families that left Gakowa with us are still in our company. Theresa Sehn and granddaughter, Julia, will go to Munich. Mr. and Mrs. Stefan Brandt will go to Regensburg near the Danube. Mr. and Mrs. Hirn have relatives in a small town near Ludwigsburg. That is where we plan to go.

We reach the city of Linz and are able to travel from there by train to Salzburg. This city in the northwestern part of Austria stands lofty and proud among its castles. It is named after the river Salzach, which winds its way through the city.

We are now close to the border of Germany and must make our last crossing on foot. We have no guide, but will follow the banks of the Salzach River. In some places, the river is quite shallow. If we could wade across it, we would reach Germany on the other side. But, the current is very strong; it will be impossible to try that with children and the elderly. We continue walking along the banks, passing trees and bushes, flower patches and rocks.

Now and then we stop to rest at places where we can be hidden from view. We hear the river rushing over the boulders, seemingly in a hurry to get to its destination, just as we are. We hope to reach the border before dark. We are strangers and have only the river as our guide.

Finally, at the edge of the forest, we see a milestone marking the border into Germany. At that point, we cross the last of the barriers. As the afternoon sun sinks behind the hills, the tall trees whisper a friendly welcome. Trees have been our protectors from our enemies as well as from the foes of nature. We are lucky to have found our way into the safety of Germany's American Zone. Everyone is exhausted but still exhilarated and anxious to continue on our journey. A bridge that crosses over the Salzach leads us into a small village where we are able to get transportation to Berchtesgarden, Germany. We arrive there in the late evening and find out that we must stay the night and catch the train to Ludwigsburg in the morning. I am excited to see that there is a public bathroom in the train station, and also a place to wash up in warm water. I let the stream of warm, soothing water trickle down my face and my arms. What luxury!

My friend Julia and I find a place on a wooden bench, snuggle up to our knapsacks and promptly fall asleep. Here we can rest easily, without the fear of being hunted down. We dream of warm beds, hot chocolate and cookies.

Berchtesgarden is a very beautiful region of Germany, with lofty mountains, meadows and alpine style houses. I am not familiar with mountains because I was born in an area of a country which is flat.

"One day we will come back here and enjoy this beautiful place," we all remark.

The morning fog hangs like a curtain before the sun and dulls the oncoming day. Restlessness and a determination to move on urges us all to check the train schedules. Finally, we board a train that takes us to Munich, about 100 miles from here.

Looking around, we realize that we are strangers in this land; not so much in appearance and language, but in our rights. Because of the many refugees who are coming into the country, there is a shortage of food and supplies. The government has issued ration cards for German citizens and registered refugees. The only way to get food or supplies is with the ration cards. We do not yet have this privilege.

"Look, Julia, those people have ham sandwiches!" I whisper.

"How I long for something fresh and appetizing like that."

"We don't have any ration cards, Kaethi, and you can't get food without them."

So we watch as the other people on the train eat their lunch of sandwiches, fruits and vegetables. We have only a few stale items of food from a few days ago. All I dream about is a fresh piece of crispy bread.

It is August 31, 1947 about noon, when the train arrives in Munich. Mrs. Sehn and Julia get off here. After our long journey together, it is an emotional goodbye. Our bond can never be broken; we are like one family. Julia cries and waves to me and I hold back tears, while calling out to her.

"Goodbye, Julia, I will miss you. Maybe we'll see each other in America."

We must transfer to another train which will take us to Ludwigsburg. While we cover miles of railroad tracks, in the fields around us farmers reap the fruits of their labors; it is harvest time. Glorious memories fill us with homesickness. My uncle Mike recalls the prosperous harvest of his own fields. The Batschka was once considered the breadbasket of Europe. It is now a wasteland under the barbaric rule of Communism.

Drawing closer to our destination, we see an increasing amount of industry. Smoking chimneys crown the numerous factories coming into sight and reveal to us the city of Stuttgart, a short distance from Ludwigsburg.

We will be going to my aunt's cousin, Lorenz Hingl and his family. He and his wife and daughter came to Germany in the early 1940's. They wanted to be able to find work in the city, because in Gakowa they were day laborers and owned neither house nor land. After serving in the German army, Lorenz settled in Ludwigsburg.

We have their address but have no way to contact them by phone. So when we leave the train station in Ludwigsburg, my uncle asks for directions to Richard Wagner Strasse 13.

"That's not far from here, sir," explains the nice lady he had asked. "Just turn right when you get out of the station and keep going until you reach the street."

"Well, we are finally here," my uncle sighs. "Let's get our things and start walking."

There is no public transportation in Ludwigsburg. Again we walk with our bundles, as we have done for the past two weeks. It is Sunday, a warm day that brings out a lot of people. They walk around, enjoying the sunshine, while we hope that our walk will soon be over.

Finally, the address we are looking for appears on the door to a three-story building. We ring the bell for "Hingl," but there is no answer. We ring again, but still no reply. After awhile, the landlady comes out of her second floor apartment.

"I am Mrs. Boehmer. Are you the relatives that Lorenz has been waiting for? He told us you were in a concentration camp and might try to escape."

"Yes, we have traveled a long way and are very tired and hungry," we tell her.

"I am sorry but Lorenz is not home. His wife is in the hospital and he and his daughter, Kaethe, are visiting her."

Mrs. Boehmer invites us in and gives us bread and jelly.

"I made this jelly from the strawberries in my garden," she tells us proudly.

A short time later, Lorenz and his daughter arrive and take us to their apartment. The reunion is joyful and excitedly we ask and answer questions back and forth.

"How long did it take you to get here and how are you feeling?"

"We left Gakowa two weeks ago. We are tired but all right," Uncle Mike replies.

We ask about his wife, Susanna, and he assures us she will be home from the hospital in a few days.

We look around their apartment. There is not much room for three more people. They have a bedroom, a small dining room with another bed in it, a very small room where their daughter, Kaethe, sleeps and a small kitchen. There is also a bathroom with a small sink. It is on the third floor and the walls are slanted like an attic. The other apartment on the third floor was bombed out and has not been remodeled.

My aunt and uncle sleep in the dining room and I become the bed partner of Kaethe. It is only a twin bed, but we make do.

The adults sit up half the night talking and sharing experiences. I am very tired and I am soon fast asleep. It's been a long time since I slept in a clean bed with a pillow and a blanket. For me, there is time tomorrow to talk to my new friend, Kaethe.

A few days later, Susanna arrives home from the hospital amid much excitement. We exchange hugs and kisses and share more news. My aunt had taken over the household chores while Susanna was in the hospital. The apartment is sparkling clean and there is a meal on the table.

In this country, all incoming refugees, either from Russian labor camps, POWs or escapees from all countries, must register. We soon find out that the nearest place for the refugees to register is in Ulm. That's where we must go to get ration cards and permission to work. That is also the place to look for relatives. We plan to go there and try to find my cousin Tobias and my father.

The day before we leave, a visitor arrives to welcome us to Germany. Mrs. Margaret Weigandt, also from Gakowa, lives in a small town near Ludwigsburg. She is a relative of Mr. and Mrs. Stefan Hirn, who had come with us from Gakowa. She just returned from taking them to Ulm for registration. She tells my aunt:

"You'd better sit down, Justina, I have some great news. I just saw your son, Tobias, in Ulm. He arrived from the Russian labor camp a few days ago and is being transferred to a farm near Ulm as a laborer."

My aunt and uncle break down in tears. We all talk at once. Questions to Mrs. Weigandt come from all sides: "How does he look? How does he feel? Where can we find him?"

"I told him you were here in Germany," Mrs. Weigandt explains, "so he will be waiting for you to come and get him."

I am wondering if we can find my father in the same camp. Although the war has been over for two years, I am still hopeful because many POWs are not yet freed.

I also wonder if perhaps my sister, Altmutter and the Findeis family, might have left Gakowa. We could trace them from here. We left the address of the Hingl family in Ludwigsburg with them, and we are now waiting to hear from them, if and when they leave the concentration camp.

The next day we leave by train for Ulm, no longer able to contain our eagerness to see Tobias. One of Lorenz's sisters, Sophie, accompanies us to help with directions. We arrive in Ulm and go directly to the registration camp. Once we register, we ask where Tobias was sent.

"Is it far?" my uncle asks. "And can you give us directions?"

We are given as much information as they have and we take off immediately. We take a bus to the end of town and then we have to walk to the farm. My uncle, who has suffered stomach problems throughout our journey, has a hard time walking. He is in great pain and cannot go any further. I am designated to stay with him while he sits by the side of the road; my aunt and Sophie continue on. We strain our eyes looking for anyone coming back our way, hoping it is Tobias. Finally, after a couple of hours waiting by the side of the road, three people approach and we can see they belong to us.

My uncle jumps up and runs toward them. Embracing Tobias, they both cry for joy. He no longer feels the pain, but is consumed with relief to have his son back. We never expected his return from Russia to be so close to our arrival in Germany.

Tobias is now 20 years old but looks much older. His clothes are mismatched and ill fitting. His shoes are scuffed and have holes on the side. He has an egg-sized growth on his cheek, which is caused by an infection of his teeth. He explains that there was no dental hygiene in the last three years, so this is not surprising. He is thin but has grown a bit since we last saw him.

I, too, am overjoyed to have Tobias back. He is like a brother to me. He, too, is happy to see me and when we tell him that my mother died and my father has not returned from the war, he tells my aunt and uncle that they did the right thing to bring me along. This is a day we will never forget.

We return to Ulm to be assigned to a refugee camp where we will be processed and checked out. We also check with the Red Cross about my father's whereabouts.

"I am sorry but there is no information on Wendel Hoeger," we are told.

Sad and disappointed, I join my relatives and get ready to be transported to the refugee camp.

We climb aboard a truck filled with other refugees and it takes us to the town of Unterjettingen. The camp is just outside of the town. We are back in the same situation, boarded together with other refugees with no privacy. However, we are free to come and go as we please. We must, however, stay until we go through processing and get permission to remain in Germany, along with ration cards and work permits.

The barracks that will house us are fairly clean, with bunk beds lined up along the walls. A low ceiling and few windows add to the depressing atmosphere of the room. The wooden floor is worn from the use during war time. We are not used to frills, so this temporary housing is met with acceptance. There is no privacy. Each family is assigned some beds and an area for their belongings. We are shown the outhouses and washing facility and the hall where food will be served to us. The daily menu is meager but adequate. Soups and stews are the mainstays of our meals. Food is scarce in Germany right now. There are so many hungry refugees added to the population and we are happy for a place to stay in a free country. We again must stand in line to register and get a pass in case we wish to leave the camp for any reason.

The fall colors resemble a sea of warmth and welcome. We often take walks by the roadside where the fruit trees provide us with extra food. We dry the apple slices to supplement the daily rations of food. I have never in my life eaten so many apples.

We meet many people with a variety of cultures and languages. They have fled their country for similar reasons as ours. We exchange stories of concentration camps, prisoner of war camps, labor camps in Russia and then begin to feel the homesickness that plagues us. Each of us has lost family members and things will never be the same. I miss my sister when I see other little girls that are the same age, and hope I will hear from her soon.

One day, Lorenz comes to visit us. My aunt's mother, who lives in Chicago, has sent a food package for us, and he is delivering it. What excitement! We open the parcel and find chocolate bars, cans of bacon, coffee, nylon stockings and cigarettes (which we use to barter on the black market) and a tin displaying a picture of a fruit cake. Excitedly we open it but find only sundries such as thread, needles, and buttons, I am disappointed, but my aunt points out that we need these items desperately. This is the beginning of many such packages.

It is now late September 1947. The days become cooler and so do the nights. We pray that we will be released soon, before winter sets in.

Tobias's Story

The days pass slowly in Unterjettingen. There is little to do but wait. I am anxious to go to school and make new friends. I am now 12 years old but have only had two years of schooling. How will I fit in with children my age who have been in school six years? Tobias sometimes helps me practice arithmetic by reciting the multiplication tables, and I write the alphabet on sheets of paper to improve my handwriting.

In the evenings, we often sit and listen to Tobias tell us about his experiences in Russia.

"How was the journey and how long did it take you to get there?" we ask him.

"We were on the train three weeks. We traveled through Yugoslavia, Romania and arrived in the city of Stalino, in the Ukraine on January 17, 1945. The food I had taken did not last more than a few days. If it had not been for some women from Bezdan, our neighboring town, I think I would have starved to death before arriving in Russia. The train was not heated, of course, and there was no place for human waste. Some of the men made a hole in the car so we could eliminate the stench. We slept close together to keep warm, wrapping the blankets tightly around ourselves. There were no windows in the train so we could not see where we were going. Sometime the train would stop and we had to get out. It was very cold and there was much snow. We were expected to stretch our legs and go to the bathroom right in the open in front of everyone. We were glad to get back in the train. Soon, dysentery set in and plagued most of us throughout the journey."

"Tobias, were you scared?" I ask him.

"Yes, I was afraid I would never see my parents or my home again. Some of the older men and women comforted the younger ones. It was hard not knowing what would become of us. When we finally arrived in Stalino, and jumped out of the train, we landed in snow hip-deep. We were definitely not dressed for this climate. Our clothing could not withstand the severely cold weather. "

After awhile, we stopped asking questions so as not to upset Tobias too much. It was hard talking about and re-living his experience. We will ask him again another day.

In October, with the proper documents and ration cards, we are finally released. Because of his time in the Russian labor camp, Tobias is eligible for double rations. This is a big help; he is constantly hungry. We are taken by bus to Stuttgart and then we board the train to Ludwigsburg, back to the Hingl family.

Lorenz has received permission from the landlord to repair and rebuild the part of the third floor apartment that had been bombed out. He has been working on this in his spare time while we were in Unterjettingen. Now everyone helps him and the place is soon habitable. There are only two rooms; a bedroom and a kitchen/living area. We must share the bathroom in the Hingl's apartment. My aunt and uncle sleep in the bedroom; I sleep in the kitchen on an army cot. Tobias is able to sleep in a room with the tenants living on the first floor, the Ott family. Because of the shortage of housing, it is a law that if a room is unused in your apartment or home, you must share it. They are very kind to him and give him a job as a parquet floor installer. My uncle finds work with the American army as a security guard in their warehouse.

Soon after we return to Ludwigsburg, a letter arrives from Austria. Altmutter writes to tell us that they have also escaped the concentration camp in Gakowa and are staying in a refugee camp near the town of Breitenhilm. Aunt Barbara, Uncle Anton, their daughter Barbara Jr. have brought her and my sister Erna along with them. They also brought my uncle's granddaughter, Katharina Rettig, whose mother is in a Russian labor camp and her father a prisoner of war. Altmutter and my sister, Erna, will come to visit us as soon as they can afford to do so. I am relieved that they are safe and anxious to see Erna. She is now six years old and will have a chance to start school from the beginning. Although we still have no news from my father, at least I know that my sister, Altmutter and the Findeis family are still alive.

CHAPTER
FOURTEEN

A New Chapter
for the
Flotz Family

While we traveled from Gakowa, through Hungary, Austria and Germany in 1947, the Flotz family was living in Csavoly, Hungary. We probably crossed paths at one time, but though we did not meet, our fate was the same.

George Jr. continues his story:

Spring 1947 and life was fairly normal for us now in the village of Csavoly.

There was church service, cultural events such as concerts, and movies. The people even celebrated their Kirchweihfest, the anniversary of the blessing of their church.

The country was controlled by the Communists. All the farms had been combined and private ownership of land had been abolished. The Hungarian Communists compared this to the Russian way of life known as *Kolhos*—state controlled. We accepted this way of life—what other choice did we have?

My father received a blacksmith shop and a small house to live in. I had been working as a laborer in the fruit orchards and vineyards and in the forest, felling trees, when a man who had a machine shop in town gave me the opportunity to apprentice with him. Shortly thereafter, though, he closed his shop and disappeared. Many other families had suddenly left town. We learned later that they escaped to Sweden and ultimately to the USA. I was disappointed to lose this great opportunity to learn a trade.

At this time, many people were escaping from the Yugoslavian concentration camps, and we realized that it would be impossible for us to return to our home in Bezdan. My father decided that we, too, should leave and go to Austria. We did not see a future in this country.

One day, after packing our belongings again, we left Csavoly and headed toward the Austrian border near St. Gotthardt. It was not heavily guarded and was known to be an easy crossing. We rode on a train with many other refugees. At each town where it stopped, the train became more crowded.

When we arrived in St. Gotthardt, the authorities took everyone into a large room in the military compound and instructed us to leave all our money and valuables on the table before us. We were warned that there would be grave penalties if we disobeyed their orders. We really had nothing more to give, certainly no jewelry or valuables. My father took out the little Hungarian money we had left and put it on the table. Our pockets empty, we were then free to leave.

The guards took us into the woods and pointed the way to the border. From here on we had to walk and carry our possessions. My mother and two brothers were unable to carry much, so my father and I had the heaviest load. One of the guards volunteered to help us. Relieved and thankful, we gave him some bundles to carry. In a while, he disappeared into the woods. We never saw him or our belongings again.

Luckily, we were able to cross into Austria safely and find a barn to rest in overnight. It was a roof over our heads, a soft bed of hay, and shelter from the rain. The next morning, we heard some voices outside; the language spoken was Croation. We feared that we had gone the wrong way and landed back in enemy territory, but we soon discovered that we had arrived in a small town inhabited by Croations who had come to Austria many years ago, as our ancestors had come to Yugoslavia from Germany. They, too, had kept their own language. They were friendly and told us which way to go.

As we made our way along the road to find the next town, the Austrian police arrived and questioned us. They could see we were refugees and told us to wait while they brought some trucks. They drove us to the town of Oberwart in the Russian Zone. From there, we went by bus to Tuln. During this trip, we passed through Vienna.

The city was occupied by the four Allied Forces, and we saw four different flags. While going through Vienna, we saw the four different flags of the United States, England, Russia and France.

We did not stop.

Once we arrived in Tuln, the refugee families were taken to farms for labor in the town of Bierbaum—again in the Russian Zone.

———————————— ✳ ————————————

Now it was summer of 1947. At age 15, I was again laboring from early morning until late at night. During the day, I worked in the fields cutting grass for hay, and then baling hay, harvesting potatoes and corn. When I came home in the evening, I was expected to feed the horses, cows and pigs, and clean their stalls.

I received very little pay for this hard work and I was getting discouraged that my life would be nothing more than hard labor. I wished to learn a trade or go to school, but this was not possible for a refugee.

Then one day, another farmer asked my father if he would let me work for him because his wife had children to care for and was pregnant besides. Again, I left my family to go to this kindly man who fed me well and gave me reasonable working hours. It was a smaller, family-oriented operation and I was the only hired hand. I felt lucky and much happier than at the other farm. In addition to a hearty breakfast, lunch and dinner, I received a snack during the morning and one in the afternoon. My working day ended in the late afternoon and I was off on Sundays.

My father was always looking for better opportunities. He went to Vienna one day that fall to check out jobs and accidentally ran into an acquaintance, Stefan Filipovich, who was from our hometown. Stefan, a brick layer, told him that the company he worked for, Illner Construction, needed iron workers. The following Sunday, we left the farm and came to Vienna. My father got the job as an iron worker, and I was hired as a laborer.

Now that I was 16, I had to work construction, which was the only work available to us refugees; we were expected to help re-build the city. I had not been to school since I was 12 years old and would not be able to further my education. I would have to become "street smart" to survive. My brother Larry was not strong enough to do construction work, but the City sponsored a youth organization into which he was accepted. He received three meals a day and training in various crafts. Eventually, he was assigned to apprentice as a fine mechanic, making instruments for doctors and dentists. This would become his life's work. My brother Johnny, now 8 years old, could finally go to school.

In Vienna we were housed in a barrack, a former POW camp that was owned by the Illner Construction Company. It was in Flachgasse 10, very close to the Schoenbrunn Castle. Besides us, there were three other families occupying the barrack, Mr. and Mrs. Filipovich, the Jost Family and the Palko family.

The barrack offered only the bare essentials—one door, several windows, wooden walls, a wooden slab floor and a roof. We had no heat or running water. At the end of the barrack was another facility that had toilet stalls as well as several faucets protruding from the wall above a trough. We had to go outside of the barrack and then enter the washroom through another door. It was very inconvenient at night, especially trying to sidestep the other people sleeping on the floor. We washed ourselves in the cold water. The toilet stalls had no doors, so there was little privacy.

At first we had to cook outside on an open fire. This was also the way to heat water to wash our clothes. Once a month we went to the public baths to get a thorough cleaning.

The men soon decided to divide the room into four sections, one for each family. Each family would have one room which also included a man-made stove. We scrounged for the materials we needed among the rubble of the city. Mr. Filipovich used his bricklaying know-how to build the stoves, my Dad made the metal top and doors and attached the stove pipes to the outside. Mr. Palko was the carpenter and he put up the walls that separated each family's room. We all helped with the things we could do, such as lifting, passing along tools and cleaning up.

Winter set in but, except for the cooking stove, there was no way to heat the rooms. We decided to gather leaves from the park and insulate the attic. It turned out to be only a temporary solution. The roof leaked when it rained or snowed, making the leaves wet and smelly. What a mess! The leaves had to go. We removed the ceiling boards and used our bare hands to push the leaves out of the attic. Soon everything was clean again.

On weekends we scavenged in the city garbage dump, hunting for the garbage that was brought from the American GI kitchens.

Their food had been shipped from America in various sizes of cans, some quite large. My father fashioned cups, pots and pans, strainers, cookie sheets and kitchen utensils. It was amazing what he could do with a few scraps of metal. Everyone in our barrack shared the household items he made. Some were sold to other refugees, bringing us a little extra income.

The Jost family, a mother and two sons near my age, and the Palko family, a couple with two daughters, blended in well with us. The young people enjoyed the sights and sounds of Vienna. We cherished the freedom to travel around the city, finding new places to see and things to do. We went to dances that were sponsored by the refugee social clubs, where we met other young people that had immigrated to Vienna from Yugoslavia and Hungary.

Soon it was Christmas. Vienna was festively decorated, and you could see in the people's faces that they anticipated the Holy Season. We had very little—but we had freedom. The Young Men's Christian Association of the local parish church hosted a Christmas party, and my friends, Joe and Tony Jost and I were invited. They served us hot chocolate, and I discovered that this was the best drink I ever had in my life. We were given used clothing. I received a jacket made out of corduroy with leather patches on the sleeves. I felt like a millionaire!

We celebrated Christmas as a family and also with our extended family—the other occupants of the barrack. We became a close-knit group and would always cherish this time. Though we were far away from our home, we were connected through our heritage.

CHAPTER FIFTEEN | Ludwigsburg, Germany 1947

A new home for us! The reunion with Tobias, my chance to go to school and a job for Uncle Mike!

Among the many new pleasures that have come to me in Ludwigsburg is living across the street from a bakery. On my way home from school, I stop to gaze at the display in the baker's window. The fancy cakes and pies don't get a second glance; I want the bread. It's been years since I tasted a crispy hard roll. The only problem is that ration cards are required for all food items and the white bread and rolls take too many stamps. *One day, I promise myself, I will be able to buy and eat as much bread as I want.*

What I really need is a new pair of shoes for school. Mine are pretty much worn out from the journey, and they are too small. One day, after my uncle gets paid from his job, my aunt and I go shopping.

I plead with Aunt Justina "Can I pick out which shoes I would like?"

"Sure, but they must be reasonably priced and of good value," she replies. "We can't afford to buy you new ones until you outgrow them."

There are not many choices of shoes for children: black or brown, simply laced, some with buckles. I look around, feeling the leather and admiring the styles. I can't remember the last time I was in a shoe store. The manager can see my excitement and lets me browse as long as I like. Finally, I decide on a brown pair with a buckle on top. I am very proud of my new shoes and promise to polish them each night so that they will last a long time. In fact, one of the evening routines is to polish everyone's shoes for the next day. My aunt proclaims, "If your shoes are clean, the rest of your clothes will look better."

My new friend, Kaethe Hingl, shares some of her clothes with me. I want to look presentable when I go to school. She is a year younger but we are the same size. The shortage of food in the past three years and my illness has slowed my growth.

We both attend the same class. I don't have the schooling to keep up with the history, geography and social sciences that the other children have learned so far, but I do well at arithmetic and language. In the German language, some words are capitalized and others are not. The trick is to learn the correct spelling and the correct usage. This is difficult and I must practice over and over each day. "High German" is spoken in schools, businesses and government, but a "low German" or dialect is practiced on the street. Each area has its own dialect, and the people of Ludwigsburg speak *Schwaebisch*. I soon pick up the dialect from my classmates at the playground, but in class we all must adhere to the correct speech.

There are many refugee children in the city, so the teachers understand. But we must do the assigned work and pay attention in class. One of the subjects I am good at is writing essays. I don't have any books to read, but our teacher, *Fraulein Staehle*, reads to us at the end of each day from a book called *Heidi*. It's the story of an orphaned girl named Heidi, so I can identify with her. I look forward each day to the next chapter. Fraulein Staehle, her graying hair braided and wound around her head like a crown, is very kind to me. Her warm smile complements her bespeckled face. She is the first person, aside from my family, who shows me kindness and takes an interest in my learning. When we have to write an *Aufsatz*, she compliments me on my skills in writing an essay. Always eager to do well in school, I am encouraged by her smiling eyes. She teaches with her heart and I believe her students mean a lot to her, an unmarried, childless woman.

Christmas 1947 is approaching. Snow falls, dressing the streets in white and harmonizing with the festive shop windows in a symphony of holiday spirit. Disappointed that there has been no news about my father, yet happy that my sister is safe, I help my aunt make Christmas cookies. Suzanna Hingl, and my aunt make oatmeal cookies using brown sugar and oatmeal, the only ingredients that are available in quantity. We shape the cookies and then take them across the street to the baker, who will bake them in his oven. Each family marks their cookie sheets with specially shaped cookies to identify them. Because we live the closest to the bakery, we smell the aroma first when they are done. Once we bring the cookies home, we carefully take them out of the pan. Kaethe and I sneak a few while no one is looking. Then they are packed away in a tin to be served at our Christmas Dinner.

My aunt's mother, Mrs. Dsida, has sent another package from America, this one for Christmas. She is a widow and lives in a one-room apartment in Chicago. It is a hardship for her to send these packages because all the money she and her husband had earned since coming to Chicago had been sent to Gakowa to build a little house for their retirement. They lost everything when President Tito disowned us. She works in a menial job during the day and baby-sits on weekends. With this babysitting money, she is able to send us food packages. The cost of the freight to send the package is almost as much as the food itself.

On Christmas Eve, we tear away the wrapping and cut open the box, being careful not to damage anything. The small boxes inside are wrapped in holiday paper and tied with curly ribbon in various colors of red and green. Little gifts for each of us—a leather belt for Tobias, a wallet for uncle Mike, some jewelry for aunt Justina and a woolen scarf and gloves for me—are tucked in among the dried fruits, nuts, chocolate bars and a few bars of fancy soap. This is not a package of necessities, but of tummy pleasers. After all, it's Christmas.

Mrs. Dsida has also sent a Christmas package for the Hingl family in appreciation for all they have done for us. We spend Christmas Eve together sharing roast beef and noodles. For dessert, the oatmeal cookies come out of hiding. Lorenz shares his apple wine, called *Apfel Most*. After a few glasses, the adults start to sing Christmas songs. We share stories about our Christmases in the concentration camp and the Hingls tell us about all the bombing they endured during the war.

Tobias is very quiet. He, too, is reminiscing about his Christmas in Russia in 1945 and 1946. After awhile, he starts to talk....

"If we didn't know it was December 24th, we could not tell it was Christmas in Russia. We did not have the day off, no special food, no signs of Christmas decorations or music. I suppose the women celebrated together by singing Christmas songs and praying for a quick return home. The barracks housing the men, however, showed no signs of celebration. We talked a little about how it might be at home; what we used to do at Christmas time in Gakowa, but no one felt much like celebrating. We were cold and hungry and no thoughts of Christmas could change that. I was 18 on my first Christmas in Russia. I had to work like a man, but my thoughts of home were those of a child."

A few days after Christmas, a letter arrives postmarked "Breiten-hilm, Austria." Altmutter has written a long letter. After the usual Christmas wishes, she begins to tell us where they are and what they are doing.

Dear Children, After we left Gakowa in late August, we spent a few weeks in a refugee camp in Hungary and then went on to Austria. We had the address of Dr. Jung, our family friend, and looked him up. He helped Anton get a job on a farm and lent him some money to move the family. We got a small room in the back of the farmhouse. Some of the neighbors gave us old furniture and household items. With six of us in one room, space is a luxury. Barbara found work on other farms in the area, sorting apples and harvesting vegetables. On her way home, she looked for pota-toes in the fields or other vegetables and fruit to bring home for supper. I walked for miles to other farms begging for old clothes. I knit slippers from the wool of old sweaters and traded them for food. Tell Kaethe that her sis-ter is fine. Because the school is so far from the farm, we are keeping Erna at home. She can start next year.

With a sigh of relief, my uncle Mike puts down his mother's let-ter. "I am so glad they have left Gakowa and are safe."

I am filled with longing. "Can we go to visit them, or can they come to Ludwigsburg?"

"We'll see," my uncle replies. "It will be awhile before we have saved enough money for the train fare. I am sure Altmutter cannot afford to visit us either at this time."

We write back immediately with our Christmas wishes. I take the letter to the corner mailbox the next day. I have enclosed a letter to my sister, hoping she has not forgotten me.

※

Shortly after Christmas, we celebrate my 12th birthday, and it is the first birthday in four years that I actually receive presents. My favorite present is a book entitled *Kleine Geschichten aus dem Maerchenland*, a collection of short stories. It's important that I practice reading to keep up with my classes. I also receive a pen and some candy. My aunt has saved some of the ration cards to buy ingredients for my birthday cake and everyone sings to me. Today I feel very special.

※

Spring 1948 thaws the heavy layer of snow that has fallen and lifts our spirits and hopes for the New Year. I am disappointed that there has been no news about my father, but am happy that my sister is safe.

School is my favorite place to be. I devour each lesson in my quest for knowledge. I have a lot to catch up. Also, I have joined a youth group and made new friends. The leader of the group takes

Ludwigsburg, Germany—This is the Stuttgarterstrasse with the park of chestnut trees on the right. My home during 1947–1949.

us on outings around the city and its surrounding parks. We learn about nature, make crafts, and sing songs. There is a castle in Ludwigsburg called *Schloss Monrepo*. I have never seen a castle. We take tours through the inside and the gardens around the castle, which has been preserved for the public. The city also has beautiful churches and museums. In comparison to my hometown of Gakowa, with one family houses, small stores, narrow streets and little to see, I am overwhelmed by this city. Even though Ludwigsburg still has a lot of damage from the bombings, there is much to see.

Close to our house is a main thoroughfare called *Stuttgarter Strasse*, where a narrow park runs parallel with the street. This park is my favorite place. Chestnut trees stand proudly row by row, leaving room for a public walkway and some benches. Spring has dressed these trees in green and adorned them with white candle-shaped blossoms. This reminds me of the chestnut trees in front of my home in Gakowa.

I am very surprised one day that a letter has arrived from Yugoslavia with the return address of my father's parents. Hoeger Opa writes:

Dear Kaethi, I am so happy to tell you that the concentration camp Gakowa has been dissolved as of February 28, 1948. Oma and I now live in Sombor, the city closest to Gakowa. We were released from the camp with the understanding that we work for the government. Oma works in the kitchen of a restaurant and I help out in the bar. I have experience from our Wirtshaus in Gakowa. We cannot leave the country. We are doing all right but miss you and Erna. With our love, Opa and Oma.

This is big news! No more concentration camp. I wonder how the town looks after everyone was released? Uncle Mike wonders what will become of the houses and the land we lost. I am so happy to hear from Oma and Opa. This is the first news from them since I left Gakowa in 1947. I sit down and write them back. I must also tell them that Uncle Mike plans to take me to America.

Now and then, I also get to go to the movies. I receive an allowance, with which I can buy a movie ticket or an ice cream cone. My cousin, Tobias, often asks me to stand in line for him to get his movie tickets. He then treats me to the movie, but I have to sit far away from him and his friends. As a young man of twenty, he doesn't want to be seen with his 12 year old cousin tagging along.

Kaethe Hingl and I spend a lot of time together. We do our homework, listen to the radio, play outside or visit some of our school friends. It's nice to have someone living right next door.

Because there is a shortage of food, Kaethe and I have to stand in line each Saturday morning to purchase the meat for the weekend. We have meat only once a week. There is also horse meat for sale. When you buy horse meat, you get twice as much for your ration stamps. We only tried that once. The meat is sweet and edible, but the thought of the animal made it unappetizing.

We eat a lot of potatoes. It's almost a daily accompaniment to any other food we might have. Many times a big pot of boiled potatoes and one small triangle of cheese is the meal for four of us.

It is now three years since the war ended, but no news has come from my father. We have checked out all the agencies responsible for finding the prisoners of war, but to no avail. My aunt and uncle have decided to take me along to America. If I am not adopted, my father could always come to claim me and my sister. Yet, we don't see much hope of finding him.

One day a letter from Aunt Theresia arrives. We all gather around the table to listen as my uncle reads it.

"What does she say?" I ask. "Can we come to Chicago soon?"

"Just be patient, Kaethi, and listen."

Aunt Theresia has begun the process of getting us to America. In order to go, someone must vouch for us, give the head of the family a job, and also provide housing. Even though the immediate families, such as mother and daughter, have priority, the rules must still be followed.

There is excitement in the air as we prepare for the trip to the Consulate. We don't have any papers, so we must bring an affidavit from someone who knows us to prove our birth date and place of birth. On the appointed day, we take the train to Stuttgart and wait our turn to be interviewed. It is a busy place. Many people are eagerly waiting to immigrate to America. We have all the proper documents and are hopeful and anxious to get approval to travel. This, however, is not to be.

"Mr. Brandt, I understand you have a minor child living with you who is not yours," the consulate begins. "This will pose a problem with your immigration status."

"But, sir, I am her guardian," my uncle explains. " Her mother died and her father has been missing in action since 1945."

"This may well be true, but we must investigate further," the consulate warns.

This man looks very stern and seems to think I should not go to America. My heart sinks. What will happen to me, if they leave me here? I begin to cry, expecting the worst. My aunt and uncle look at each other and with a firm voice, my uncle decides:

"We cannot leave without Kaethi. Please tell us what can be done to allow her to accompany us."

The man's face softens as he realizes the sacrifice my family is willing to make. He turns to my aunt and explains:

"She can go with you but not on the 'priority basis' which you would be entitled to as a daughter of an American citizen. You must, therefore, wait your turn along with the other applicants who want to immigrate to non-relatives."

We thank him and depart. I am grateful to have such caring people who will not leave me behind. I hug my aunt and uncle and thank them. We arrive back home in Ludwigsburg and my aunt sits down to write a letter to her mother, explaining what happened. We are disappointed but hopeful our emigration will not take too long. Sadly, it takes almost a year.

CHAPTER SIXTEEN | Going to America

It is a happy day in August 1949, when the postman brings the news that we can pick up our immigration papers in Stuttgart. Aunt Theresia has made our travel arrangements easy by buying us plane tickets. This must have cost her a lot of money and I am very grateful that she has included me.

It is decided that before we leave, my sister Erna should come to visit me from Austria. Altmutter has written that she will bring Erna to Ludwigsburg to say goodbye once more. We have been separated for two years. The only hope I have is that once we arrive in America, we will be able to help Erna, Altmutter and the Findeis family immigrate.

Anxiously looking down the railway tracks, I spot the oncoming train bringing my sister and Altmutter to Ludwigsburg. I wonder how tall Erna has grown, and if she will be speaking in an Austrian dialect. I am impatiently looking up and down the windows of the train but see no one resembling my eight year old sister. Finally, I see the conductor helping an elderly lady and a child down the steps of the railcar.

"There they are," I shout excitedly. My uncle has already seen them and goes to help with their luggage. I run to meet them and embrace my sister. She is shy but remembers me and finally gives me a big hug and kiss. The last time we saw each other Erna was only six, so I can imagine that she feels a bit awkward towards me. I then greet Altmutter. She is only 57 years old, but she looks much older. She hugs and kisses me while tears run down her face. "How proud your mother would be of you two girls," she whispers, while tears continue to flow.

My uncle tries to change the mood. "Come, Mother, stop crying. We are very happy to see you both." He guides us out of the train station to begin our walk to Richard Wagner Strasse, the street where we live.

Erna and I walk together holding hands. She looks tired but I encourage her to walk fast and we will soon be home. I tell her that I have a small gift for her. In one of the last packages Aunt Theresia sent from America were several chocolate bars, one of which I saved for Erna. She smiles with anticipation and I know we have broken the ice.

We arrive home; Mrs. Hingl has prepared a meal for us, a favorite dish of mine called *Dampfnudel*. The dish is made from raised dough formed into dumplings the size of a small fist. They are placed in a pot in which brown sugar has been melted with a little butter. The dumplings are steamed until the dough is cooked and the sugar is a little burnt resulting in a glaze for the dumpling. Before eating a dumpling, we roll it in the sugar glaze. There is also some salad that the landlady, Mrs. Boehmer, donated from her garden in honor of our guests.

My sister and I spend a lot of time walking around Ludwigsburg. I show her my school, the church, the parks and the castle. In comparison to the small town of Gakowa, this city is overwhelming to her. "I love the castle and the flowers in the park." While we walk around, I ask her if she remembers much about Gakowa and the camp. "I don't remember too much, but can't forget the long journey to Austria," she says. "We often walked for miles and I could hardly keep up."

Erna tells me about her life in Austria. "I sometimes go into the woods with Altmutter to pick berries, which she sells at the farmer's market in *Graz*. I love being in the woods, looking for all kinds of wildflowers while I search for the berries. Altmutter is a very good saleslady."

"Do you have to walk far to get to school?"

"Now that we moved to Graz, it's only half an hour, but when we lived on a farm near Grambach last year, we walked almost an hour to the nearest school. It was very cold in the winter."

I ask about her grades and she announces proudly: "I got a very good report card. Now I am going to 2nd grade when we return home. I was not able to start school when we arrived in Austria in 1947 because it was too far to walk and I was undernourished and small for my age. Aunt Barbara thought it best to wait a year."

One day I see Altmutter whispering to my aunt and uncle in a corner of the room. My curiosity peaks when I hear her say: "Shouldn't we tell Kaethi and Erna?" Then my father's name is mentioned. I fear that they know something about our father and I ask them to tell us.

"I was informed by a man from Gakowa, who also served in the German army in Budapest, Hungary, that he saw your father there," Altmutter tells us. "Your father worked in the field office with the army because he had some experience in office work.

It was spring of 1945 and the Russian and German armies fought a fierce battle in the area. The Russians surrounded Budapest and none of the German soldiers ever came out alive."

"Are you sure, Altmutter, that he died there?" I ask. "We have not been notified by the Red Cross."

"Child, this happened four years ago and I am sure he would have been found by now." She is careful to avoid any details of his death and burial.

As so many times before, Erna and I are beyond tears. We have waited so long but are almost glad to finally have the answer. Our lives will be guided by our aunts, uncles and, of course, Altmutter. At this moment, it occurs to me that my father must have died around the same time as my mother, neither of them knowing about the other's fate. It is probably best that way.

One day, Altmutter decides that we should have a portrait taken before we are separated again. We pick out our best dresses for this occasion. Aunt Justina washes our hair and braids it in a special way. At the studio, the photographer poses us in different settings. The camera and the lights fascinate us while we wait for his cue. The one position we like best is where we sit next to each other. We don't know when we will see each other again.

While we wait for the photographer to set up his shots, I remem-

Erna and I and Kaethe Hingl pose for the picture in
Ludwigsburg, Germany, before my journey to America in 1949.

ber the last time we sat for a portrait. It was in 1944, before my father left for the army. My mother had sewn new dresses for Erna and
me. We took the train to Sombor, the nearest city to the photographer's studio. We looked sad on the pictures. The smiles which the
photographer tried to coax from us did not appear on our faces.

"Erna, do you remember when we took the last picture together
with our parents?" I ask my sister.

"No, I can't remember."

"I forgot, you were only three years old then," I recall.

The memory of having our family picture taken reminds me of
the time when Erna was born. I begin telling her about it.

"Erna, before you were born, I wanted a baby sister or baby
brother so badly that I would sing the folk song: '*Storch, Storch gut-
er, bring mir a kleiner Bruder, Storch, Storch bester, bring mir a kleine
Schwester.*' That song asks the stork to bring us either a brother or
sister. As children, we were told that that's where the little babies
come from."

Erna listens and smiles: "Did you really do that?"

"Yes, and I had to wait six years for you. In 1941, when Mami was pregnant with you, I contracted scarlet fever. I was taken to Altmutter's house because this disease was very contagious and Mami could not be exposed to it. I was very lonesome for her and Dadi, but Altmutter and Altvater tried to make me comfortable. Mami would come and stand by the window, calling to me and waving, which made me feel even more lonesome. I wanted her to come in and sit by my bed, but that was impossible. She would bring me little gifts and cookies, but that did not take her place.

Finally, on September 22nd, you were born and Dadi came to tell me. I was overjoyed and could not wait to see you. Shortly after your birth, I was well enough to come back home. When Mami bathed you in the wooden tub, I was able to help. I finally had a sister to play with. At that time, I did not realize how important you were going to be to me."

As Erna listens, she smiles and we hug and cry a little. I feel she should know how happy I am to have her.

The time has passed quickly. Erna and Altmutter must return home to Austria. "You take care of yourself," Altmutter cautions us, as she tearfully says her farewells. Erna is crying because now she realizes that we will be separated again. She has become quite at home here with us.

"Can I come to America, Uncle Mike?" Erna asks timidly. He assures her that as soon as we get settled and can get a sponsor for them, we will all be reunited again. We hope that this promise will become a reality.

Again, we walk the same route to the railroad station, carrying their suitcases. The train has pulled in and we help them up the stairs. Altmutter and Erna lean out of the window and as the train starts to move, Erna waves with one hand and brushes away a tear with the other. Her braids are flying in the wind. Soon we see only Altmutter's white handkerchief fluttering like a bird. My cousin Tobias brushes away my tears. "Come, Kaethi, I'll buy you some ice-cream," he comforts me as we leave the train station. I am once again reminded that I am cared for by a loving family.

———————————— ✳ ————————————

While preparing for our journey to America, one subject that touches me deeply has upset me.

"Kaethi, girls your age don't have long braids in America," my aunt counsels me. "We must cut your hair."

Since I lost my hair during my bout with typhoid fever four years ago, I have considered the beautiful thick growth of hair a special blessing. I don't want to lose it.

"I'll look so different with short hair."

"We'll go to the beauty parlor where they will transform you into a young lady. We will ask them to save the braids for you," my aunt proposes.

Reluctantly I accompany my aunt to the beauty shop. Why do I feel like I am losing a friend or a treasured toy? The beautician asks me to sit in her chair and puts an apron-like gown around me. She smiles and assures me that I will look wonderful. I am not convinced. I close my eyes as she begins clipping my hair. I shudder with each snip of her scissors. I am trying to hold back my tears, but I feel the wet droplets running down my cheeks.

"All done, open your eyes, Kaethi," the beautician announces. "How do you like your new look?"

As I open my eyes, she hands me a lock of my hair to keep.

"I must admit, it's not so bad. It will take getting used to, but I do like it."

This is a big change in my life—the braids of the little girl are gone and the new hairdo of the young lady is here. Those braids remind me of my life in Gakowa with my family; the camp, where I lost my hair from typhoid fever, and then regained it again. It is the end of one part of my life; and my new look will be the future in America.

We begin preparing for our journey. My last day at school is bittersweet. I have learned much in the two years with Fraulein Staehle, my favorite teacher.

"Kaethi, I hope you will write to us. Good luck in the American school," she tells me, her smile ever so loving.

"*Auf Wiedersehen, alle miteinander,*" I wave a farewell to all as I leave the room.

I walk down the Stuttgarter Strasse one more time, admiring those beautiful chestnut trees. It is September—the ripened chestnuts have fallen to the ground and the squirrels are busy hoarding them for the winter.

Kaethe Hingl, my constant companion, and I have shared so many good times together. I will miss her. She promises to write and I return that promise. We bid farewell to Frau Boehmer, our landlady who was first to welcome us to Ludwigsburg two years before. Our neighbors wish us well also, when we tell them that we will leave soon.

One of the last things I do is write a letter to my sister, Erna.

Dear Erna, This will be the last letter you receive from me for awhile. We are going to America in a few days. I had my hair cut—it looks different but I am getting used to it. I am very excited to fly in an airplane. Imagine sitting in a seat while flying in the air! I will tell you all about it when we arrive in Chicago. Don't be sad about our leaving. Uncle Mike has promised to bring you all to America as soon as we are settled there. By then I will know how to speak English and I can teach you. Be good and do your best in school. I know it will be your birthday soon, and we all wish you a Happy 8th Birthday. Give my love to Altmutter, Aunt Barbara, Uncle Anton and Cousin Barbara.

The day before we depart, we enjoy one more dinner together with the Hingl family. Yes, it's Dampfnudels again. The Hingls have given us a place to live, shown us around Ludwigsburg, helped get jobs for my uncle and Tobias and helped me with school work. We will always be grateful to them. We reminisce about the good times we shared during the past two years and enjoy each other's company one last time. Tomorrow we leave!

On September 17, 1949 our journey to America begins. The train ride from Ludwigsburg to Frankfurt is scenic. It is harvest time again. We see the farmers in their fields just as we did two years before. We pass through many towns which are new to us. We will probably never see them again.

We will be flying out of the international airport in Frankfurt. I am a little nervous. I have never seen an airplane up close, let alone ride in one. We stay overnight in a modest hotel near the airport. To pass the time, we attend a movie and then eat out in a small coffee shop. This is a special treat for us.

The next day, we leave on a TWA plane bound for New York. Before the boarding call, there is an announcement calling my uncle to the desk. Once more he is questioned about me. The Children's Services want to make sure that I am safe and not taken away against my will. They tell my uncle that their representatives will contact us in America and check on me several times a year.

The loudspeaker announces our flight and we walk up the steps to the huge machine that will take us across the ocean.

As I look out the window of the plane, the skyline of Frankfurt in my view, many thoughts cross my mind. I am reminded again of the happy days spent with my parents and sister in the first nine years of my life. I cannot forget the next three years spent in the concentration camp; my bout with typhoid fever, the death of our mother, the loneliness, fear, and hunger, the final goodbye of my home as I escape with my aunt and uncle and journey to our destination in Ludwigsburg, Germany. Fourteen years of my life are gone. I have lost both of my parents, my education, and part of my childhood. I hope for a better future as the wheels of the plane lift up and we soar into the sky.

The Flotz Family in Vienna

T he Flotz family's life has become structured now. Going to work, going to school, going to church and having the freedom and a little money to seek entertainment and friendships is a part of their life. George, Jr. continues his story:

I was 16 and working with my Dad at the Illner Construction Co. We still lived in the barrack with the Filipovich, Palko and Jost families. Housing for refugees was scarce.

At that time, we worked to rebuild and enlarge a factory on the outskirts of Vienna. We had to take a train to the site. Trucks brought the sand and the bricks to the work area, but the various jobs such as mixing the mortar and getting the bricks to the bricklayers up high on the scaffolds were done manually. No machinery was available during that time. There were troughs in which the cement, sand and water were mixed by hand using a hoe. The water was carried in buckets from the nearest well. Rows of men and boys stood ready to pass the buckets of water down the line. Once the mortar was mixed, it was poured into buckets and pulled up by a rope to the bricklayers, who emptied the mortar into a container and returned the bucket for more. The bricks were hurled up to the bricklayers with a paddle one at a time. These men were quite experienced in their task. Sometimes, the bricks missed the hands of the workers and fell back down. We always watched for falling bricks. The catchers had no gloves, but caught the bricks with their bare hands.

My friend, Joe Jost, and I worked as laborers. My father was assigned to the iron work because he had experience in that field. Soon my father developed a hernia, which disabled him for a long time. After surgery, it took a few months to recuperate before he would be able to return to heavy construction work. Meanwhile, I was now the only breadwinner in the family.

It was difficult for a 16 year old to work all week and then turn over most of his hard earned money to support the family. There was not much left for me to spend on myself. In my free time, I picked a sport that was fairly cheap. I went mountain climbing on weekends. A backpack filled with water and a little food accompanied me on the weekend tour through the mountains around Vienna. On these tours, I met other young men and developed some good friendships. We stayed in youth hostels in the mountains. While walking the trails, we met other hikers who then joined us. No one had much money. We made up for it by singing songs and telling stories around the fire in the evenings.

I enjoyed my weekend outings very much. It was a relaxing time in the outdoors, away from the daily chores at the construction site. When I walked along the mountain trails high above the world below, I felt exhilarated. I wanted to forget the cramped living quarters in the barrack, the stifling hot conditions during the summer, the absence of privacy and the destruction around us. Nature in its glory: lush green meadows with grazing herds of cows and sheep, tall evergreen trees grouped in rows and rows of forest, snow-topped peaks blazing in the sun, small houses built precariously on the hills, a vision of peace—I was happy.

---------------------------- ✳ ----------------------------

In the fall of 1948 my father finally returned to work. I had been looking for other opportunities and talked to my friend Joe about it.

"Did you see the poster down the street advertising the French Foreign Legion?"

"Are you serious?" Joe replied, surprised.

"It looks really glamorous. The men have nice uniforms, they travel the world, they get paid well and we could get out of the barracks."

We discussed our dream repeatedly but told no one about it. We went to the Legion Office and checked out the facts. We liked what we heard and so we applied.

"What is your mother going to say?" I asked Joe.

"She will be upset. All she has is my brother and me."

We were accepted a few months later and then told our families. After a long discussion, they felt that maybe this would be good for us. So, during the next few days we prepared to leave. We did not tell our boss about our venture; we just did not return to work the next day.

Joe and I walked to the train station to report to the French Foreign Legion. We walked slowly and were deep in thought. As we stood on the platform of the train station and looked out around us, I slowly turned to Joe.

"Are we crazy? How can we leave our families and go off to a strange land?"

All at once we grabbed our bags, dashed out of the station and walked home. We laughed and agreed that neither of us wanted to back out because it would seem cowardly. We were both relieved that we came to our senses in time. Our families were happy to see us.

As time went on, opportunities to work in places other than in construction opened up for refugees. There were good paying jobs in the oil fields around Vienna; however, the Russian army controlled these jobs and you had to be a member of the Communist Party. This I passed up quickly.

I finally found work at a wallpaper factory appropriately called *Wiener Tapetenfabrik* (Wallpaper Factory of Vienna). I was on a team that worked on reconstructing the wallpaper for the Opera House, which had been bombed. This company had made the original paper and still had the mold. The paint had to be mixed exactly to the original design and printed in the two-foot by two-foot mold. This process was repeated over and over again and took a long time. I was proud to be involved in such an important job. I promised myself that when it was finished, I would attend the Opera and survey the beautiful walls.

While working in the factory, I befriended many locally born young men. There was a union at the factory which sponsored employee activities. During the summer months, outings into the union-owned hostels were very popular. I participated in each outing; hiking and mountain climbing was my favorite activity. The union also had a club room where we could meet during the evening hours in bad weather and in the winter. There were ping pong tables, card games, or you could read the daily newspaper or books. I was very interested in educating myself. I could not attend school, but read everything I could get my hands on. The daily paper provided me with current events—world news and sports. I approached some of the local boys and asked them to bring their unwanted books to the club room. We leased out the books for a small fee and then bought new books with the money. After a few months, we had quite a library.

---------------------------- ✳ ----------------------------

One evening, as I was coming home from work, my little brother, John, came running to meet me. I wondered why he was so excited.

"Guess who came to visit us, George?" he called out.

I guessed that it might be our uncle Simon, my father's brother. I was right. Hurriedly I went to greet him. We had not seen him for a long time. He looked very thin and tired, but Uncle Simon was always full of good humor. He smiled and greeted me warmly:

"How are you, George? I have missed you and the whole family."

We exchanged news since we saw each other last and I asked about my aunt Maria and cousins, Franz, Simon and Seppi.

"They all send their good wishes and hope to come to Vienna soon. I am here to look around for a job and a place to live."

We all sat down to supper and Uncle Simon told us how he came to Vienna. He lived in the Steiermark (another Austrian province) which was occupied by the English. The entire area surrounding Vienna was occupied by the Russians. No one could penetrate the Russian zone from other areas. So he took a train to the end of the English zone, then walked through forests and crossed over a mountain to bypass any border patrols. He was successful in getting into Vienna unnoticed. We admired his courage and stamina to walk over a mountain to reach us.

My mother had made a vegetable soup, which Uncle Simon ate with great gusto.

"Anna, you could always make the best soup."

With the little food we had to make this meal, this was a particularly worthy compliment. She smiled and thanked him.

After the meal, we asked him many questions particularly about our Flotz Oma, who remained behind in Bezdan when we left in October 1944.

He paused a moment and composed himself.

"You haven't heard anything, have you?" he said.

We told him that no news had come from her.

"She would not leave Bezdan with you, Anna, so when the Russians came into the town, she was raped. She was 80 years old. Someone from my family was a witness. She overcame that horror but was soon put into the concentration camp in Gakowa, along with my wife and boys. When my boys were hungry and cried for food, Oma would sneak out at night, past the guards, and walk to Bezdan. She still had some friends there who were Hungarian and not taken to concentration camps. She begged for food from them. One night, it was bitter cold outside; she could not bear it any longer and found a shelter in a deserted shed. She froze to death that night. A few days later, some people found her. They, too, had been begging for food and had sought shelter in that shed.

She was brought back into the camp in Gakowa and buried in the mass graves."

The atmosphere in the room became very quiet. My father wiped away his tears and could not believe what he just heard. We were stunned that this terrible fate happened to our Oma.

"She should have come with us," my mother uttered in disbelief. "She would have had a better chance of survival."

Uncle Simon left after a few days, promising to come back with the whole family. My father was visibly moved when he left. This was his only living brother. He looked forward to having him close by.

Although things seemed to be getting better in the country, a year later, we were still living in the barrack and had no hope of an apartment. Housing was very scarce. Young couples getting married had no choice but to continue living with either set of parents. This was true for the Viennese citizens as well.

We heard a lot of people were immigrating to America. Those who had relatives to sponsor them had the advantage. My father's brother had gone to America as a young man in the 1920's but he had died there. We heard that there were relief organizations that sponsored people. This would be our way to go.

I approached my father and mother about going to this new land.

"I have no desire to leave Austria, now that my brother Simon and his family have come to Vienna," my father argued. "I don't know English and am not accustomed to their way of life."

"Dad, please reconsider," I countered. "We could have a house one day, if we work hard and save our money, and Johnny could learn a good profession."

All my arguments did not persuade him. I was very anxious to go and decided to go alone. My mother would not hear of it. I guess she must have talked to my father and pleaded with him to give his sons the opportunities that would be possible in America. It took some time, but eventually, he agreed. I was overjoyed.

We went to see the American Consulate in Vienna. They arranged for our family to immigrate through the sponsorship of the Catholic Relief Organization. We applied and waited.

Meanwhile, the Jost family also left for America. As fate would have it, my friend Joe married Marie, one of the Palko girls in our barrack. Their final destination was Chicago.

It was late November 1951. We received notification from the American Consulate that our papers had been approved. We were asked to come into their office. My father and I, wearing our best clothes, took a bus to the middle of the city where the Consulate's office was located. Through the hustle and bustle of the snowy day, we were in good spirits, hoping to hear good news. We entered the building and took the elevator to the third floor. The hallway was long with doors marked with the names of the various offices. Finally, we reached the door marked: "American Consulate." To our surprise there was a sign posted which read: *Geschlossen zum Danksagungstag.* It was the fourth Thursday of November and the Americans were closed for Thanksgiving.

A little disappointed, we returned home and went back the following week.

"Your papers are ready and you can leave for Salzburg as soon as possible," the young man explained. "From there, you will be put on a train with other refugees going to Bremen. In Bremen, you will have to wait a few days until there are enough passengers to fully load the ship.

"Thank you very much, we are ready to go," I told the kindly gentleman. He seemed truly happy for us and wished us good luck on our journey.

My mother and brothers were very excited when we arrived home to announce our good fortune. Little did we realize how hard our journey would be until we reached America! Before we left, my friends at the youth organization celebrated with me. It was a bitter-sweet parting. I did enjoy my life in Vienna and my good friends, but I knew there was no real future for me here.

"Don't forget us, George," they reminded me, "you will have to come back and visit sometime."

"I will always remember my friends and the beautiful mountains," I told them a little sad at that thought. It would be quite a long time before my return.

I gave notice at the wallpaper factory and said my farewells to my co-workers. I had learned a lot about making wallpaper. "Good luck, George, we hope you have a good trip and success in your life in America," said my boss and he added a hearty handshake.

I thanked him and left, buttoning my coat and putting on my cap to keep out the brisk winter wind that welcomed me on the street. I had closed the door to my life in Vienna and anticipated the sweet dreams only the young can conjure up.

The Flotz's are
Going to America

The day has come when the family prepares to go to America.
George, at 19, is full of anticipation. Times will be hard at
first, but he is willing to try his hand at anything in the new
country. He tells us about the journey...

We packed our belongings in a couple of cardboard suitcases.
The little furniture and kitchen items we had were left for the other
families in the barrack. We had been together four years in these
cramped quarters and had grown as close as a big family. We were
sad to leave them. They wished us well and promised to follow us
to America.

Early in December, 1951 we left on the train to Salzburg in Austria. There, we made the connection with the refugee train to Bremen in Germany. The weather had turned cold and it snowed. The
holiday season was approaching and the atmosphere was one of anticipation, not only for Christmas, but for our new home far away.
Would we be in America for Christmas? I wondered if Christmas
was celebrated the same as in this country. I supposed there were
church services and a good meal and hopefully presents. But, surely
we could not expect much this year.

The train ride to Bremen afforded us new sights in Germany.
Now we were riding in a passenger railcar, not a cattle car, which we
were forced to use in 1945. We were comfortable and enjoyed talking to the other refugees, who were all anticipating better and hap-

The Flotz Family on their way to Bremen before boarding the ship for America, 1951.
From left: George Jr., George Sr., Larry, Anna and Johnny.

U.S.N.S. GENERAL STUART HEINTZELMAN (T-AP 159)

The Flotz Family was carried to America on this ship.

pier lives in America. We arrived in Bremen the following day. Our overnight quarters were assigned to us by the Catholic Relief Organization staff that sponsored this trip. We were given food and drink and asked to stay in the area. We did not know when the boat would leave, but were told that once enough people were here to fill it, the journey would start.

"Great news," my father announced a few days later, "I have been told that we will be on the troop ship General Heinzelman which will leave tomorrow." He was right. Soon we were asked to volunteer for various jobs on the boat. This was a free trip but everyone had a job to do. I volunteered to be a security guard. We were taken on the boat right away to familiarize us with the accommodations, the safety measures and the mess hall. I was anxious to see what a ship looked like and felt very important to be part of security. The first thing that impressed me when we got to the ship was, of course, its size. What a majestic structure! We arrived on board and the fragrant smell of coffee greeted us. I never had American coffee made from coffee beans before. I drank so much that I got a little sick.

We were told that our job would be helping people find their quarters; supervising the mess hall; policing the gangways to keep the passengers away from the crew's quarters, and watching for the safety of the children on deck. We had no weapons, but received an armband signifying our security status.

When we boarded the next day, everyone was excited. My 12-year-old brother, Johnny, was wide-eyed and amazed at the size of the ship. We were assigned bunks in the sleeping quarters a few stories below deck. There were no portholes. Men and women were separated. The adults slept on the lower bunks and the young people and children had to climb up to the top. It was fun climbing up but I was hoping that I would not fall out when the ship was bounced around by the waves. It didn't happen, thank God.

The journey began from *Bremerhafen*, the port of Bremen, on December 8, 1951. The slowly departing vessel blew its whistle as a last goodbye to the waving crowd on shore. We had no one to see us off, but we waved to everyone. The ship held 1,214 passengers, over five hundred of which were *Statenlos*—without citizenship to any country. This was our status, too. We belonged to no country but hoped to be new citizens of America. The non-military crew running the ship was hired by the United States government. All the labor on board such as cook's helpers, cleaners, security and various odd jobs were assigned to the passengers, who traveled free of charge.

So began a two week journey that I will never forget.

The day after we departed, I was doing duty on deck when I saw a most spectacular sight—The White Cliffs of Dover in England. I had seen the movie starring Greer Garson in Vienna and was familiar with the scenery. We were only about a mile away from shore so it was possible to see the white-marble rocks jutting out of the ocean. It had impressed me during the movie, but did not compare to the real thing. I quickly called my family so they could witness this once-in-a-lifetime moment. I had seen my first new country and its famous landmark.

It wasn't long before my mother and Johnny became seasick. They could not make it to the mess hall, so I tried to bring them some food even though this was not allowed. A lot of the passengers became seasick; many of them had to be taken to the dispensary for care. The ship had a doctor and nurses and was pretty well equipped to handle emergencies, especially seasickness.

The December storms wielded their wrath upon the ship. The vessel tossed back and forth, up and down; waves crashing across the deck. Some days, the captain had to slow down the speed to prevent the ship from tossing around so much. The General Heinzelman was built as a military troop ship and could withstand the storm, but the captain felt sorry for the passengers, most of whom suffered seasickness. I was able to handle it pretty well, but soon even my father and brother Larry succumbed to this awful feeling of nausea.

Amid storms and calm weather, we passed our time doing duty or relaxing in the community room. In the mornings, there was a kindergarten for the smaller children and in the afternoons, on certain days, we were able to watch movies. Everyone had to rise at 6:30 A.M. We had to make our beds, pick up clothes or towels lying around, sweep the room and clean the bathrooms. There was strict discipline in these matters and inspectors came each day to see that order prevailed. If they found that things were not in order, certain privileges, such as movies, were curtailed.

The place reminded me of "Noah's Ark." Instead of animals of every species, there were people of almost every nationality speaking many languages. Each group sought out its own. We listened to the people around us and when they spoke in German, we immediately made contact. I met some young men, my little brother Johnny found friends who spoke his language, and my parents made friends with adults who were, like us, coming from Austria and Germany's refugee camps. We felt blessed, like Noah, to be safe on a vessel taking us to freedom. No matter how badly the storms attacked our oasis at sea, we had faith that we would arrive in a safe harbor.

One day, while on duty near the kitchen, one of the cooks started talking to me.

"My name is Charlie. I speak a little German," said the portly man with a wide grin as he extended his hand in greeting.

"*Gruess Gott*, Charlie," I answered while returning the handshake.

Charlie did pretty well in German. He told me he came from Brooklyn, New York.

"Brooklyn is a special place, George; it's got a collection of the population of the world. There are Irish, Germans, Italians, Polish, Russians and also a variety of religions," Charlie explained. "Come and see me sometime."

"I don't know where we will end up," I mused. "We must go where we find work and a place to live."

I often saw Charlie while on duty, and he would tell me what was on the menu for the day. The food we were served surpassed anything we had eaten in a long time. There was meat every day. Along with the tasty stews, meatloaf, roast beef, and hamburgers, we were served fresh vegetables, fruits and plenty of bread. It was easy to gain a few pounds—if you were lucky enough to be able to eat. As the days passed, the weather calmed down and with the help of the pills given out to the passengers with seasickness, they were able to keep their food down.

If America was anything like this, we would be happy.

Each day, we received the "General Heinzelman News." It was an attempt to bring information to the passengers. In it, we learned of the number of passengers on the ship, their nationalities, their religion and their gender. There were reports of news around the world as well as weather reports. The rules and regulations of the ship were posted and we received updates of the journey's progress. Most important, there were instructions about our duties before departing the ship in New York. It was necessary that the ship be cleaned from top to bottom; walls had to be washed, the bedding stripped, garbage collected, the floors scrubbed and all items packed up or discarded.

One day, almost two weeks after our departure from Bremerhafen, we saw a flock of seagulls flying over the ship when the garbage was thrown overboard. We knew we would soon see land. On December 21, 1951, late evening, we entered the harbor of New York. Because it was already dark, we did not see the Statue of Liberty, which I had looked forward to seeing. At the time, the statue was not lit up at night.

We saw a few small lights blinking in the harbor, but everything was closed up and we had to stay on the ship for another night. We had been told that the port authorities would come on board in the morning and handle the customs duties right here.

This was a big project as each family had to be processed once more and given the final authorization to enter the United States—our green card. After each family received their proper documents, they were allowed to debark.

As we walked off the ship, tall skyscrapers greeted us from the distance. We were tired and anxious and wondered what awaited us in the new country. The New York harbor was a busy place. Tugboats moved in and out pushing the big ships into the harbor. There were cargo ships and passenger ships all lined up waiting to load or unload their goods. There was a ferry, which we later found out went from Staten Island to Manhattan. Coming from a small town, we could not imagine how this ocean traffic maneuvered safely.

We arrived in a large hall housing all the immigrants. We were designated to a place where the Catholic Charities Organization would meet us. There were many religious organizations that sponsored immigrants and each group had their own spot.

We were met by a young man, smiling widely and gesturing for us to follow him.

"Welcome to America! Please come over here and wait."

We stood in line waiting for the representatives of the various factories and corporations to pick out workers for their places of business. We felt like we were at a slave market. The young single men and women found favor with the "lookers" first. They were alone and had no families as baggage. As people were picked around us, my father began to worry.

"What's going to happen to us if no one chooses us?" he worried.

"Will we have to go back?" my mother cried.

I felt responsible, because it was at my urging that we came here. I tried to comfort them. My Dad was 48, my brother Larry 21 and I was 19. Couldn't anyone use three men?

The day ended with no luck. The young man in charge of our housing took us by bus to an old hotel, provided us with sandwiches and milk and left us until the next morning. We did not sleep too much that night. How could this happen? Didn't we look good enough to be part of the American work force? I tried to calm my mother and told her that surely tomorrow we would find someone who needed us.

The next morning the young man came to pick us up and, again, we stood in line as if we were at a horse market, trying to look our best. Naturally, our clothes were worn and wrinkled from the journey, but we were ready to work. Do you know how demeaning it is to be looked at and judged as unfit? Sadly, we were overlooked again. Our bus ride back to the hotel that night was even more depressing.

By our third day in the harbor, only a few people were left. No one came to hire anyone this day; it was December 24th—Christmas Eve. I don't remember how it happened, but we were put on a bus and told that we were going to a chicken farm in Freehold, New Jersey, where a farmer needed help. We couldn't argue, and had no choice but to bundle up our belongings and leave.

Late afternoon, we arrived at a bus station outside Freehold. The bus driver motioned to us to get off and most likely told us to wait for someone to pick us up. We didn't understand him, yet assumed as much from his gestures. We sat at the lonely bus station for a couple of hours. It had gotten dark. Because it was Christmas Eve, few people were in the station. There were decorations on the wall and Christmas music flowed from the loudspeakers. "Silent Night" is understood in any language. We were overcome with homesickness and despair. How would this end?

Finally, a pickup truck arrived. It wasn't hard for the driver to recognize us. We looked tired and sad; our eyes showing anxiety and hope that he was our ride. He smiled and helped us get our baggage into the truck. He motioned to us: "Come with me. My name is Joe and I work at the chicken farm."

We followed eagerly, anxious to get settled somewhere. About an hour later, we arrived at the farm. The lady of the house, Mrs. Roth, showed us to a small cottage next to the main house, where we were to live. She didn't seem too friendly; however, she brought us some eggs, milk and bread.

"*Danke schoen,*" my mother said as she smiled and accepted our supper.

Mrs. Roth spoke a little German and told us about our duties for the next day. We all looked surprised that she would ask us to work on Christmas.

"Tomorrow is Christmas, Mrs. Roth, can we go to church?" my father asked.

"There is no Christmas for you," she told him gruffly. "In America you must work and have money before you can have Christmas off."

Deeply disappointed and hurt, we accepted our fate. She wished us good night and left. My mother prepared us a meal of scrambled eggs for our Christmas Eve dinner and we quietly went to bed. This Christmas was the bleakest we ever had. Here we were in America, the land of freedom and plenty, and yet we were denied church service and a holiday off.

Later, we found out that Mrs. Roth was Jewish of Polish descent; her family had been killed by Nazis during the war. We could understand her resentment towards us because of our German heritage.

The chicken farm had 50,000 chickens. Thank God the feeding process was mechanized. We still had to be there to work the machines, but the belt-driven conveyors moved automatically in front of each chicken coop. However, water had to be brought to each group of chickens. The eggs were picked by hand. They were separated by size and color by an automatic conveyor. Then they were washed and sanded manually. After that process, they were packed in egg dividers and sent to the distributor. It was a full day's work for each of us. Even Johnny was helping. We were paid $2.00 per person per day and given our housing plus all the eggs we could eat and a few chickens a week. The rest of the groceries we bought ourselves.

My mother was an expert at preparing meals with eggs in most unusual ways. She made noodles in different sizes and thickness. She fixed noodles with potatoes, noodles with cheese, noodles with jelly, noodles with cabbage, noodles with cream of wheat. She filled square noodle dough pockets with a variety of fillings. Of course, there were scrambled eggs, poached eggs, eggs over easy, hard boiled eggs and eggs fried with noodles. Surprisingly, I still like eggs.

A few days after we arrived, Mr. Roth came home from a trip. He seemed very friendly and hospitable and was happy to see that help had arrived for the farm work. The couple had no children, and Mr. Roth became particularly fond of Johnny.

One of the nicest things he did, as I remember, was to give us a ride to town in his car. He took us to the corner drug store and bought us a chocolate malted. We sat at the counter, watching the soda jerk scoop vanilla ice-cream into a tall metal container. He added chocolate syrup and slipped the container in an electric mixer that made a lot of noise. Once mixed, he poured the delicacy into a tall glass and topped it with whipped cream and a red cherry. He stuck a straw into it and ceremoniously put it in front of us. We never had anything like this in our lives. It smelled delicious and looked like a snow-topped mountain in Austria. We were experiencing our first "teenage occupation"—sitting at a soda fountain in an American drug store.

"How did you like your chocolate malted?" asked Mr. Roth. He smiled as he realized how fast we drank our treat.

"Thanks very much, sir, we loved it," I told him and my brothers agreed by eagerly nodding their heads; Johnny rubbing his tummy.

"I'll take you for a ride through town," said Mr. Roth. "You can see all the beautiful houses and gardens and the stores on Main Street."

We sat back in his car and watched other cars go by, admired the store windows and longingly looked at the nicely kept houses and lawns we passed. Would we ever own such a house? When we arrived back on the farm, we told our parents what we saw and the treat we had at the drug store. They were pleased that Mr. Roth liked us, and we got to see so many things in town.

Not far from the farm was the Nestles' chocolate factory. Aromatic fragrances wafted our way on days when the wind came from that direction. I wanted to work there! This was my first love affair with chocolate. I often sat outside the cottage and waited for this aroma to come drifting my way.

Life in America for the Flotz Family

O nce here in America, the Flotz Family strived to better themselves. As all immigrants experienced, it was not easy. The
first thing to do was to learn English. Everything else would
come in time. George Jr. continues to recall life in New York. As fate would
have it, though, his quest for a new life would soon be interrupted.

In February 1952, while still working on the farm in Freehold,
New Jersey, we heard from my mother's sister, Theresa, and her family who had immigrated to Queens, New York. She asked us to come
live with them and find work in New York. We knew that $2.00 per
day would not be enough to give us a decent life in America and my
brother, Johnny, needed to go to school. We left the chicken farm
and moved to Queens.

My father and brother Larry found work in a machine shop,
and I was hired in a printing shop. At that time, we printed post-
ers for the election of Dwight D. Eisenhower, who was running for
president of the United States. We also made the buttons with "Ike"
printed on them. My whole family and I wore those buttons proudly, and I told all my friends that I was working for the future "president."

My brother Johnny, now 13, finally went to school again. He
made friends and learned English faster than any of us. He helped
me with my homework from night school, which I attended several
times a week.

I had to start in first grade English class. The lessons were simple English and I practiced doing homework on the ride to and from work. I found the spelling of some words different than they sounded such as "Wednesday" or "language." Johnny and I often laughed together at our pronunciations of these words. Eventually I graduated from first grade at the end of the school year but did not return the following year. I tried to read and teach myself by reading the newspaper. This way I also learned about the government and business in the United States.

I loved New York—the bright lights in Times Square, the magnificent Empire State Building, the fun and games at Coney Island, the dancing Rockettes at Rockefeller Center, a subway ride—all were exciting for me. One of the first things I did was visit the Statue of Liberty, which I missed at our arrival. When I arrived on Liberty Island where Lady Liberty proudly lifts her torch, I could see that she was facing out to sea. How appropriate! Her inscription, written by Emma Lazarus, welcomes the many immigrants who are arriving now:

> *Give me your tired, your poor, your huddled masses,*
>   *yearning to breathe free*
> *The wretched refuse of your teeming shore.*
> *Send these, the homeless, tempest tossed, to me*
> *I lift my lamp beside the golden door*

I stood in awe of this beautiful statue, sent to America by the people of France in 1886. I wanted to see more and walked up into the crown on her head, where little windows give you a breathtaking view of the area. I was overwhelmed by my emotions. If this statue welcomed me, I must be home.

I also joined a choir called "The Austrian Youth Choir." I attended German dances and met many young immigrants. Six months after arriving in America I was required to report to the draft board.

Later in 1952, we moved away from my aunt to an apartment building in the Bronx. We received a free apartment in the basement next to the boiler room in exchange for cleaning the building and firing the boiler. The apartment had heating pipes running along the ceiling. The windows were high up and when people walked by, you could see only their legs. The noise from the boiler and the popping of the heat going through the pipes became a constant accompaniment to our daily routine. My mother did the cleaning and

World's Tallest

hoto Made Atop Empire State Building, New York 1952 1250 feet
102 stories

The Flotz Family visiting the Empire State Building in 1952.

my father and my brothers and I shoveled the coal and pulled out the ashes. We were still able to keep our day jobs, so the free apartment was a bonus.

Then in April, 1953, *Uncle Sam* "pointed" to me. I had been drafted and ordered to report to Ft. Dix, New Jersey for four months of training in heavy weapons. My life as a free man was over again.

The day I was to leave, my father accompanied me to the bus at the draft board. It was the first time I saw my father cry.

"It seems unfair that you have to be exposed to danger again, after all you have been through during the war in Europe," my father cried. "You are not even a citizen."

"It's all right, Dad, there will be many like me in the Army. It is the law. If we want to have freedom, we must fight for it."

He hugged me tightly and turned to leave. He turned once more and waved. I was touched by his unusual show of emotion.

I boarded the bus along with the other draftees going to Ft. Dix. After a couple of hours, we arrived at the base and were assigned our bunks. Life became measured in orders—get up, eat, march, train, and go to bed. I met another German immigrant, Martin, with whom I became friendly. Both of us had trouble understanding the complicated instructions of the machine guns and equipment. Without the benefit of schooling, I had barely learned English, let alone understand the technical terms. The Army, however, did not allow for this disadvantage. If we could not do what was expected, we were penalized by getting our passes voided or getting KP duty.

I often wondered why the sergeants barked their orders at us and insisted on the "Yes, Sir" after each answer given. I would have obeyed their orders had they asked nicely. The constant marching at all hours of the day and night with your full gear on our backs surely prepared us for the hardships of war. It is often said that the Army "makes a man out of you." I guess I should have been used to the harsh treatment from my time in Europe during the war, but you never get used to abuse. I followed the orders as best I could and tried to learn the army language for the weapons, clothes and food.

"Let's get some chow," my buddies would say. I found out that meant dinner. A particularly unpleasant name for one of the meals was "shit on the shingle," toast with hamburger meat and gravy. The first time I heard "fatigues," I thought they were talking about being tired, but I learned soon enough they meant my clothes. When training with guns, you had to specify if it was a pistol, a rifle or machine gun. In fact, since I was not too excited about handling guns, I had a problem during training. I would always hold the gun on my shoulder, but away from my face. One day, the shot backfired into my cheek and left its mark in the form of a good size swelling. Did I take some ribbing from that! I made friends fast and they helped me understand. The training was hard, yet there had to be a good reason to condition us to save ourselves from harm.

At the end of the training period, sometime in July 1953, we were told that President Eisenhower would come to Ft. Dix for the induction of citizenship upon all of the immigrants serving in the army. Small groups of soldiers of many nationalities—German, Italian, Polish and French—arrived in camp after their basic training was over. The ceremony was planned for a large group of men, so it took a little time to get enough soldiers together. The President wanted all immigrants serving in the United States army to be citizens. I was very excited to be able to get my citizenship and tell my parents. They would be so proud of me!

After we waited a few weeks, an announcement was made that this plan was cancelled. We never found out why, but it was not to be! We immediately were processed for shipment to various destinations. It was all done according to the alphabet. Persons with names A–E went to Europe, F–Z were destined for the Far East. I was crushed. Coming over on the boat from Germany, we would hear news about war in Korea. Who would have thought that I would one day be going there to fight?

I came home for a week of leave before shipping out to the West Coast. My parents were very upset that Korea was to be my destination. I did not want to fight in a war, but the thought of seeing the Far East interested me. I wondered what it would be like in Seoul or Japan, a totally different culture than mine.

Meanwhile the Korean War, or Police Action, as it was called, ended July 27, 1953. We were going there on a peace-keeping mission and to rebuild Korea. But it was still dangerous. There were mines all around and snipers attacking, and we had to deal with prisoners of war. I hoped there would be a place for me serving in capacities other than shooting. I hated guns and wanted no part of carrying one around with me. I was to find my niche as soon as we arrived in Korea.

I reported to the train station in New Jersey for the journey to Ft. Lewis, Washington, located near Seattle. It seemed that trains had been part of my life in the past few years. I was seeing America from one end to the other, which I never could have done at this time in my life. At 22 years old, I was traveling the world. We had Pullman cars with porters. We slept in bunks and ate in the dining car. The scenery, which showed me all of America from the East Coast to the West Coast in the fall of the year, has become one of my most pleasant memories. First we saw the Midwest with flowing rivers and fields of wheat and corn, then prairies of Iowa, Nebraska and Oregon. Finally in Washington State the mountains and small towns reminded me of Austria.

Upon arriving at Ft. Lewis and being assigned to our quarters, the process of physical and mental readiness began. We received our shots, were examined by doctors and opticians and received many papers to fill out. After finally completing this rigorous duty and leaving the building, I was told by an officer that I had just volunteered for duty in Korea. I was stunned because I didn't remember volunteering for anything. He explained that UN rules permitted only "volunteers" to go to the Far East. I could not argue with that.

We went to Korea by boat via Alaska. Here I was again on a transport ship, with the memories of the boat ride to America still very vivid in my mind. The weather was calm, however, and the journey quite comfortable. We were assigned various jobs to do on the ship. I had volunteered for kitchen duty. I enjoyed cooking. I came from a family with all boys, so I often helped my mother in the kitchen. Thinking that the experience received on the ship might help me further my kitchen duties when we arrived in Korea, I became an avid learner. A young soldier from New Jersey named John Fritsch became a close friend. He was also a German immigrant and we hit it off right away. He worked with me in the mess hall. We cooked for about two thousand soldiers. I was glad that I was only a helper and not responsible for the whole meal. The kitchen area on the ship was well equipped with deep fryers and grills as well as large pots and pans. We had to eat in shifts to accommodate everyone in the mess hall. There were no tables to sit at, merely raised platforms to hold one's plate. We had to stand while eating.

When we approached Alaska, the view was spectacular. Water and mountains covered in white met in dramatic panorama. It was a stark resemblance of wilderness. I was in awe. We landed in Juneau and some of the soldiers disembarked for duty there. The rest of us went on to Korea.

Our journey through the Gulf of Alaska took us past the Aleutian Islands and on to the Bering Sea. After about ten days, we landed in Sasebo, Japan where we were briefed again and, in exchange for our Class "A" uniforms, given fatigues, combat boots, weapons and instructions. We also received sleeping bags and survival kits —ready for the foxholes. We were shipped to Pusan, the southeastern port of Korea, in LSD's (open trucks on water). I belonged to "D" company, 34th Infantry Regiment—24th Division—8th Army. The "D" Company was the machine gun squad.

My view of the country was not as shocking because I had seen devastation in Germany and Austria. Some of my friends, however, found it hard to accept. The Koreans lived in appalling conditions. Their housing was merely "a roof over their heads," shacks, consisting mostly of cardboard, showed no signs of sanitation, neither running water nor sewers. The smell of smoked fish cooking on top of

The Flotz Family during George Jr.'s visit from the army in 1953.
From left: George Jr., Anna, Johnny, George Sr., and Larry.

make-shift stoves took your breath away.

My expectations of the Far East were much higher than the reality. There would be other places worth seeing in the northern cities of Korea, I hoped.

We were housed in shacks that once held prisoners of war. The walls were built of various sizes of stones. There was no mortar between the stones to close up the holes, and the wind blew right through it. The roof was made of metal sheets, and when it rained, a cascade of rushing water disturbed our sleep. There was a dirt floor that turned to mud during the rainy weather. It was primitive but no worse than how the locals lived.

We were patrolling the area to check for mines and snipers. It was now close to Thanksgiving. The weather turned chilly and damp. When it rained, the whole camp was one large mud puddle. We were allowed to attend religious services of our own faith. My friend John was Protestant and I was Catholic. I attended his services and he came with me. After the service, we usually got coffee and cookies. This was a good way to keep warm, and so we soon started to go to all the various services, even the Jewish one. It was usually pretty dark in the tents and you were not recognized easily. Soon, however, our little scam was detected by the chaplain and he restricted our church-going to one service a week. Well, we tried...

I was truly amazed when we were served Thanksgiving dinner. We had shrimp cocktail, turkey, stuffing, and sweet potatoes—the works. The Army really outdid itself by shipping over all the trimmings for this holiday. I never had shrimp. I tried some but they did not agree with me. I got pretty sick. I never had turkey either and was surprised at the taste. We were all a little homesick by now and this sign of "home" helped us overcome our loneliness. After dinner, someone had a mouth organ and soon voices joined in the old familiar tunes.

Soon after Thanksgiving, a large fire broke out in the area where the locals lived. Most of their shacks burned down. The Army was commissioned to help rebuild Pusan. This was our job for the next few months while we waited to be called to action. We replaced the shacks that had burned with wooden ones which were more stable.

In January 1954, when the job was completed, we were moved north to the Yanggon valley to camp "George." Could the Army have named the camp after me? What irony! Our mission there was to continue the daily patrols for mines and snipers for the safety of the area.

When digging our foxholes, we sometimes found the bones of Korean soldiers. While on a hill, we radioed for food, but in the infinite wisdom of the Army, the helicopters brought us sand bags. We ran out of water. Some guys volunteered to go down the mountain to get water. It took one day to go down and one day to return. The water was contaminated, but we had tablets to purify it.

I got tired of the daily marches up and down the muddy hills, carrying equipment that equaled my body weight. I was looking for another way to serve. I found it in the mess hall. The cook was being rotated home and they were looking for a replacement. My friend John Fritsch and I volunteered immediately. They told us that we needed to go for training in Seoul. John left first and then I was to follow when he returned. But while he was gone, I became mess sergeant. I loved this work. I had to be up early to prepare breakfast for three hundred men, but it didn't bother me. I loved baking pies in the middle of the night and decorating the mess hall to make it more like home.

I had a special feeling for the Korean children who came daily to beg for food. The shoe was now on the other foot. I was able to give instead of begging or stealing. When I thought back on the times that my brothers and I walked a long way to find food to survive, I was happy to give these children our left-overs. They even took our garbage to feed their animals.

Then in June 1954, we were transferred to Ascom City—American Military Base. There we lived in Quonset huts and had a more normal life. I celebrated my 22nd birthday in Yong Dong Po near Seoul. There was a Club for G.I.'s and I spent my whole month's paycheck of $73.00 for the party. I invited all my friends and filled the whole Club. It was a little part of heaven for a few hours.

Our unit handled the prisoner of war exchange. The prisoners were assembled in a part of Panmunjom (No Man's Land) called Freedom City and given a choice of returning to their homes or staying with the captors. 50,000 Chinese prisoners chose to stay with the UN and 28 American PWO's chose Communism.

During the summer of 1954, I received an order to go to Seoul for my citizenship. I needed two witnesses who knew me well. Everyone wanted to come with me just to get away to the City. But, the officers had first choice. They, of course, did not know me as well as the other soldiers. During the proceedings, the officers were asked my name. They answered "George." That's all they knew about me. One of the questions they asked me was: "Are you a Communist?" I told them "No" and thought about the absurdity of asking me such a question. Thankfully, I received my citizen papers and was now an "American" soldier. The date was September 2, 1954.

"Congratulations, George, you will make a fine citizen," the officers told me.

"Thank you, I will try my best, and thank you for coming with me," I answered proudly. I took them to the nearest bar and we celebrated. It was a great day in my life.

When we returned to camp, my friends were waiting to celebrate with me.

In November 1954, our unit was moved back to Sasebo, Japan. During one of my leaves I was able to visit Nagasaki and Hiroshima, the cities on which the atom bomb was dropped. Again, I saw total devastation. It looked as if a giant foot had stepped on a box of toys and leveled everything into tiny pieces.

My friend, John Fritsch, who worked with me in the mess hall, was diagnosed with possible T.B. while we were in Japan. He was taken to Yokohama to a hospital. I visited him and found him in an "iron lung." I'll never forget that day. Seeing him lying in this metal box really scared me. He looked at me with very sad eyes and an expression of hopelessness.

"John, this is no way to get out of the Army," I joked with him. He smiled and I think he felt better.

"George, I am so scared. I don't know what will happen to me. My girlfriend Rose and I are planning to get married when I return."

"Things often look worse than they are. Just keep up your spirits. I'll come to see you again."

"Will you please write to Rose for me, George, and tell her where I am."

Things did work out for John and he recovered. He then was shipped stateside and I never saw him again, although we have kept up with annual Christmas cards.

We received good news that, because we served in Korea, our two-year duty was cut short by two months. I was released in February 1955 and boarded the troop ship "Sultan" along with thousands of other soldiers going home. When we passed through the Golden Gate Bridge in San Francisco, I stood on the deck and proudly entered the United States a second time, although from the opposite end of the country. My thoughts were of my future. What would I do with only a fifth grade education? I learned English while in the Army and knew how to cook for a big crowd, but it was not my intention to pursue that.

I was released from the Army as a corporal on March 8, 1955. Soon thereafter I arrived back in New York in my parents' apartment. After I rested a few weeks and spent some time visiting my friends, the family suggested I go to Chicago looking for work. We had many friends from our hometown of Bezdan there, and my parents wanted to be close to them. I agreed and took the train to Chicago.

This city was big but not as congested as New York. I came to the South Side of Chicago known as the Hyde Park area. There were large apartment buildings, wide boulevards, the University of Chicago and the nearby lakefront. It was definitely less crowded. The friends I stayed with lived and worked in the apartment building in which they did janitorial work. This kind of work was usually done by the new immigrants.

While staying with one of our friends, I looked for work and found a job at U.S. Rubber on the 2–10 P.M. shift. After receiving a couple of paychecks, I moved to the YMCA. In those days, there were no fast-food places or stores open that late at night, so I had to resort to canned tuna or sardines and crackers for my supper. Luckily, I was invited to Sunday dinner at our friends' house, which I appreciated and enjoyed very much.

In those days, it was hard to find an apartment, so it took me awhile to find one large enough for my parents and my brothers and me. I tried the north side of Chicago and was lucky to find a two-bedroom apartment on "George" Street. It was a far cry from "Camp George" in Korea. I called my parents with the good news and they immediately made plans to take the train to Chicago. I met them at Union Station, excited to see them again and show them their new living quarters.

"George, how did you manage to find this place?" my mother asked, as she looked around the apartment. I could tell she was pleased by the smile on her face.

"I am glad you like it. This is in the "German" neighborhood so you will find other immigrants and stores that sell foods with which you are familiar," I told her.

Her face lit up when I mentioned the neighborhood and ethnic food stores. She was pleased with my choice and walked around from room to room exploring the possibilities of the new furniture placement.

Soon my Dad, now 52 years old, found a job at a machine shop. My brother Larry worked in a factory, and 16-year-old Johnny went to high school at Lane Tech. He also got a part-time job in a grocery store. We were together again.

I was not happy at U.S. Rubber. The fumes bothered me and the late shift restricted my social life. One of our friends, who worked at Jewel Food Stores, suggested I apply there in the meat department. I was hired and spent three years as an apprentice, learning on the job. I attended school for meat cutting on my day off. After three years, I graduated to journeyman butcher. Since I had some experience cooking, I was often asked by the shoppers how to prepare certain cuts of meat. Those ladies loved me! Unfortunately, because I had no education in America, there would be no advancement in the company. I could go only as far as assistant manager, which I eventually achieved.

My $50.00 per week salary was shared with my family. The $25.00 I had left for personal expenses left no savings for a car. However, while in the Army, I had saved my money, and together with my Dad and brother we were able to buy a home within one year.

Another young man from Bezdan, Frank Kaufmann, lived near me and on Saturday nights we took the bus to the Lincoln Turnerhall on the north side of Chicago and attended the various German dances. At this time, many young immigrants spent their time there because it cost only $1.00 to get in and you could dance all night. The drinks, of course, were not included, but I was never a drinker, so a soda would do. Many young people met their mates during those events, and Frank and I had our eyes out for some cute girls.

CHAPTER TWENTY | *Arrival in Chicago 1949*

My journey begins with an airplane ride that starts out with excitement and anticipation but I soon find myself in a state of nausea. I must endure this condition all the way to Chicago.

I don't know if it's my anxiety about flying or if the propeller-driven plane cannot control the air pockets and wind gusts, but I am very uncomfortable and air sick. Ever since take-off, my stomach is turning topsy-turvy. My aunt and I sit next to each other and we both feel very nauseous. Uncle Mike and Tobias are sitting in front of us with no problems. The stewardess is constantly feeling my pulse and checking my forehead; I guess I look pretty sick. The plane is fully occupied and others complain about the air sickness; yet I am their worst case.

We arrive in New York on September 19, 1949. While waiting for a connecting flight to Chicago, I am glad to have some steady ground under me. In the airport, I see signs advertising *Coca-Cola* and I ask for some. I don't like the taste, and it upsets my stomach again. But I discover a vending machine with chewing gum. Excitedly I ask my uncle for some change. The coin drops in and a white and green package of gum falls out of the machine. My first experience shopping at a vending machine proves to be a lot of fun.

The airport is crowded and noisy. Since I don't feel well, I miss the sights that most newcomers stare at in amazement. Tobias tells

Theresia Dsida, my aunt's mother, who brought us all to America.

me to look out the windows and see the skyscrapers, the planes taking off and landing around us. I just want to close my eyes and sleep.
I hope I don't die before we arrive in Chicago.

The flight to Chicago arrives at Midway Airport in the late evening. As we approach the city, the sea of lights below us resembles
a toy city with toy cars and toy people. It's hard for me to look out,
but everyone insists that I surely don't want to miss this glorious
sight. My first look at Chicago is so overwhelming that tears well up
in my eyes at the sight of this enormous panorama.

"How can people find their way around this big city? How will
this airplane ever find a place to land?" I muse as I stare out in be-
wilderment.

Happy to see the end of our journey, I sit back and wait for the
plane to stop and the doors to open. The captain announces the
landing procedures and we settle back, waiting to touch down. We
are finally here!

The international airport building is busy processing immigrants and visitors alike. It takes a little while but soon we are free to
walk into the waiting area of the airport. As soon as we enter, greet-

ings are shouted in our direction and a group of people converge upon us.

It has been many years since my aunt has seen her mother. We all stand back and let them greet each other. Aunt Theresia is a little woman, just like her daughter. They joyfully embrace—tears and hugs and kisses. Much has happened since they saw each other so it will be awhile before they can catch up on all the news. Aunt Theresia has never met her grandson, Tobias. And of course, she has never met me.

"I am so happy that you are finally here. How are you Tobias? This must be Katherine," are the excited words coming from Aunt Theresia's lips.

I give Aunt Theresia a hug and tell her thanks for helping me come to America. Her warm smile tells me that she is happy I came.

I finally recognize someone. Uncle Stefan and Aunt Appolonia Brandt, my grandfather's brother and sister-in-law who left Gakowa with us and traveled with us to Germany, are here to greet us. They had been able to come to Chicago on a priority basis last year because their daughter and son-in-law, Eva and Joe Dsida, are citizens of this country. We embrace warmly, happy to see them again. Their daughter, Eva, hugs me and says:

"Katherine, you look a little sick. Can I get you anything?"

"Thank you, I feel better now, but I did not like the flight."

There are more friends of Aunt Theresia's greeting us. They have come to help with our luggage. As we leave the airport, I am surprised to see that everyone came in a car and we are divided up into groups and taken back to Uncle Stefan's apartment for dinner. Since it is dark now, I cannot see much of the city, but I am a little scared of all the cars on the highway. Uncle Stefan lives on the south side of Chicago and it takes only about half an hour to get home.

I am not sure where we will live, but soon find out that we are all staying with Uncle Stefan and Aunt Appolonia because Aunt Theresia lives in a one-room apartment and has no room for us. Uncle Stefan is a janitor and lives in a one-bedroom basement apartment in the building where he works.

As we enter the apartment, going down three steps, I see that there is a large living room with a couch and some chairs and a radio, a dining room with a hide-a-bed, table and chairs, a small kitch-

Aunt Justina and Uncle Mike, in 1947, before coming to America.

en and bath. Of course, the bedroom is for Uncle Stefan and Aunt Appolonia. There are heating pipes overhead, a normal thing for a basement apartment.

"Make yourselves at home," invites Aunt Appolonia. "I made some chicken soup for you."

The aroma of the soup penetrates the apartment as we enter. The table has been set and I spot a bowl of fruit with oranges and apples. My eyes widen. I ask if these oranges are for us. I recall having gotten a few oranges for Christmas as a child, before the concentration camp. That had been a delicacy reserved only for Christmas.

"Help yourself, Katherine, eat as many as you like," I am told by Aunt Appolonia.

All of us sit down to a tasty bowl of chicken soup with noodles. The hot soup soothes my stomach after the uncomfortable journey. For dessert, there is ice cream, a delicacy we all love. I also eat an orange, slowly peeling it as I used to do as a child. This way it lasts longer.

After dinner, one of Aunt Theresia's friends takes her back to her furnished room on Kimbark Avenue. She has to go to work the next day, but Eva promises to come back tomorrow. She will help us get situated.

My cousin, Tobias Brandt, in 1947 before immigrating to America.

"Why don't you call me Aunt Eva?" she offers as she is leaving. "I am the same age as your mother and I am her cousin, so it's all right."

I graciously accept. I see a definite resemblance to my mother and feel the warmth and love she exudes towards me. She is only one year older than my mother. I am drawn to her kind smile. Aunt Eva tells me about the nearest school, a place their daughter, Julia, attended. It is a Catholic grammar school and will require a tuition payment. I don't know who will pay for that, but I am told not to worry about it.

The next day, Aunt Eva takes me to the school office for registration. Since school started a month ago, I will have a lot of catching up to do. Before we go to register, she takes me shopping to buy some clothes. I get to choose an outfit for the first day of school. A white blouse, a red and white checkered, pleated skirt, white sox and penny loafers are the items in our shopping bag. Thankful and excited, I show off the clothes when we get home.

The school requires uniforms, but for the first impression, I am dressed in new American clothes and shoes. A little scared, I walk up the steps to the principal's office with Aunt Eva. We are welcomed by a smiling nun who already knows Aunt Eva. It takes a few minutes of introduction and information, and I am whisked into one of the eighth grade classes.

"This is Katherine Hoeger," Sister announces to the class. "She just came from Germany and will not understand us for awhile. I hope you will try to help her and be kind to her."

The boys and girls smile at me curiously, as all 14 years olds will do. I sit in the back of the room, but the next day, Sister puts me in the first row so she can give me a little more attention and help.

While I spend my days in school, my aunt helps Aunt Appolonia around the house and Uncle Mike and Tobias become acquainted with janitor work by helping Uncle Stefan and Joe Dsida at their jobs. They mop the vestibules and vacuum the hallway carpeting and they learn a little about fixing plumbing and electric. Also, fall has brought down most of the leaves, which must be raked and burned. Uncle Mike has already applied to the union steward for a job, and Tobias has a possibility of becoming a janitor's helper in a big high-rise building near Lake Shore Drive. Aunt Justina will be looking for a job as a cleaning lady. As soon as Uncle Mike gets a 'home building' in which the janitor receives a free apartment in the basement, we will be moving out.

A few weeks after I start school, the girls tell me about the upcoming October 31st holiday called Halloween. I am curious what that is all about.

"Halloween is a day when we dress up in costumes of famous people or movie characters and knock on doors to ask for 'trick or treat.' The treat is usually some candy, which you put into the bag you carry along with you," the girls explain to me.

The older boys and girls often play tricks by throwing eggs or spray-painting the doors with shaving cream. My eighth grade classmates invite me to join them on Halloween. I don't have a costume but the girls dress up as clowns or witches. They seem more interested in the "tricks" rather than any treats. I am not comfortable watching the tricks that are played on people. It's amazing to me that you can do all these things in America and not get arrested. I soon decide to go back home.

The girls who live near our block often walk home from school with me. They chat amongst themselves and I listen carefully, trying to understand what is being said. I have picked up many English words and phrases that the teens use, and I often join in. The nuns and the students are most helpful. I receive special attention and help from the homeroom Sister, but she appoints a different girl each week to explain the homework to me.

Soon the grocery stores display pictures of a strange-looking bird and signs asking you to order your turkey early. I have never seen or heard of a turkey and wonder how it will taste. We are invited to Eva and Joe Dsida's home for Thanksgiving dinner and Eva explains:

"When the Pilgrims arrived in America many years ago, they celebrated with the Indians in thanksgiving for the bounty of the harvest. We continue this celebration each year on the fourth Thursday of November."

We arrive at their apartment to the succulent smell of roast turkey, fresh bread, colorful vegetables and salads. We also get to meet their daughter, Julia, who has come home from college for this holiday.

The table displays their beautiful dishes and glassware. An arrangement of dried wild flowers rests in the middle. Even the napkins have a picture of a turkey in colorful feathered dress. Candlelight reflects in the freshly polished silverware.

A bowl of fresh fruit, dishes of walnuts and a box of chocolates catch my attention. I think of my little sister, Erna, and wish that I could bring her some of these delicacies. It's been a long time since I saw a whole box of chocolates just standing there for me to enjoy.

"I hope you like turkey," Aunt Eva exclaims, as she proudly carries in the main meal. "These orange-colored potatoes are called sweet potatoes, and there is stuffing made from meat and spices. The red, fruit-filled, molded salad is called 'jello' and there will be pumpkin pie for dessert."

We all try a little of everything and find it to be very delicious. I like dark meat and ask for the drumstick. When I realize its size, I am a little embarrassed, but I can always share it with someone.

We have experienced our first Thanksgiving in America. We thank the people around the table for all their help in bringing us to America and the bounty we have shared.

In a way, we are pilgrims as well.

During the meal, a light snow begins to fall. By the end of the day, a major storm has developed, covering the roads and sidewalks in snow. There is no holiday for the janitors, so the four men leave to shovel the first snow of the season.

The next day, I sit down and write to my sister in Austria:

Dear Erna, You won't believe what we ate yesterday. It is called turkey —it's something like a chicken, only much bigger. A funny looking salad mold, which jiggles when you pick it up with your fork, turned out to be a challenge to eat. It is called 'jello'. It tastes fruity and when you put it in your mouth, it feels like a rubber ball and soon melts. There is a holiday called Thanksgiving when you come together with your family and friends to eat and eat. People buy fruit and cookies every week. You don't have to have a birthday or anything. I hope you can soon come to America. Next month will be Christmas and Aunt Justina told me that she will be sending a package for you, so please look out for it. Be good and behave. Love, Kaethi

As soon as Thanksgiving is over, preparations start for the Christmas Play at school. Of course, I am not chosen for a speaking part, but Sister invites me to be part of the choir. Some of the Christmas songs, like "Silent Night" and "O Come All Ye Faithful," are also sung in Germany, so I am familiar with the melody. I just need to learn the words. We practice during music hour and sometimes after school as the date of the play nears.

At home, we prepare the Christmas packages to be sent to Austria and to Germany. My sister is getting some warm sweaters, mittens and a hat. We also include chocolates and a small doll. Some canned meats, rice and barley, and dried fruits for the rest of the family go into the box as well. It's expensive to mail packages to Europe, and we don't have much money, so the gifts are small. A small package also goes out to the Hingl family in Germany in appreciation for their help in housing us there.

We are still living with Uncle Stefan and Aunt Appolonia. It is a little crowded, but we have a lot of fun preparing for this Christmas. Aunt Eva often comes to visit and help her mother. Aunt Appolonia has a heart condition and is not feeling well. She does not complain but often retires to her bedroom to rest. One day, shortly before Christmas, Aunt Eva and Uncle Joe bring a Christmas tree for us. They also give us some of their decorations for the tree. Glass balls of every color, strings of colored lights and silver tinsel, along with a little angel for the top, all add to the finishing touch of the tree. Now we are ready for Christmas.

The day has arrived for the Christmas play at school. The auditorium is filled with anxious and proud parents, grandparents, aunts and uncles. Aunt Theresia also makes time after work to come and see the program. The nuns are great at keeping order in the waiting areas, and we stand nervously waiting for our turn. The usual crib has been set up, Joseph and Mary standing over the baby Jesus, "angels" dressed in white and shepherds in long brown robes surround the scene. The choir sings beautifully, to the delight of the audience. My heart is full of reverence and joy at this scene. But I am overcome with homesickness for my parents and my sister. Memories of a quieter Christmas surrounded by family outshine this beautiful Christmas pageant. I am reminded of the beautiful church of St. Martin and the rousing organ music at Christmas. I was old enough to come to Midnight Mass with my parents, walking briskly in the freshly fallen snow. It was a long way from our house to the church. Bundled up in warm clothes, boots and woolen hat and mittens, I kept pace with my parents who held my hands, keeping me safe between them. I am grateful to be here, but my heart aches for my home and family.

"Katherine, you look so festive in your choir gown," Aunt Theresia tells me after the program has ended.

"Thank you. I feel like an angel in this long, white gown with the red scarf around my neck."

After the program has ended, we all go back to the apartment for coffee and cake and everyone remarks how much they enjoyed the beginning of the Christmas season.

Soon letters of Christmas greetings come from Europe, one of them from Altmutter. Erna, now in second grade, has scribbled a few words at the bottom of the letter.

Dear Children, We hope you have found work and are settled in Chicago. We now live in the city of Graz. Anton works at a construction site and Barbara is cleaning houses for the American soldiers' wives. She brings home food and old clothes for us, which is a blessing. I take care of the house for the family. We have only two rooms for the five of us. Erna must walk about half an hour to school. The church is next door to the school. Erna is preparing for her First Communion in the spring and one of the ladies, for which Barbara cleans house, has offered to buy the white Communion dress for her. This is wonderful news because we could not afford anything to dress her properly. We hope you have a wonderful Christmas and we thank you for the packages you sent us."

"Froehliche Weihnachten to all," writes Erna and draws the shape of *a heart underneath.*

One day, after coming home from school, a large brown envelope sits on the dining room table with all the other mail. It is addressed to me and the return address tells me it is from Ludwigsburg. Frauelein Staehle, my former teacher, has written to me. But, when I open the envelope many letters fall out. To my great amazement I see names of my school mates at the bottom of the letters. I can't believe it, the whole class wrote to me for Christmas. I am very homesick at this time of the year and especially miss the many friends from school in Ludwigsburg. The whole evening is spent reading. I cry and I laugh at some of the things they write me. What a wonderful surprise!

Uncle Mike has begun to work as a janitor at some small buildings, but none large enough to supply an apartment for us. Aunt Justina has found work housecleaning, so we are all busy each day.

Our first Christmas in America is spent at church services and then at a festive dinner with the whole family. Aunt Justina prepares the roast and vegetables, while Aunt Eva brings cookies and cake. Aunt Theresia has brought some fruit cake and ice cream. We exchange our gifts, mostly new clothes. I look forward to more gifts for my birthday only three days after Christmas. I will be 14 years old.

After the Holidays, Aunt Appolonia takes a turn for the worse and on January 28, 1950 she dies. This is the second time in my short life that I have been a witness to death. After the funeral, I have a hard time passing the bedroom where she died. However, in order to get to the bathroom, I have to go past that room. I am terrified. I am afraid to look into the room for fear of seeing her body. I sometimes ask that somebody go with me. They laugh at me, but I am very afraid. It takes awhile until I become comfortable passing the room.

Soon Uncle Mike gets the good news.

"What luck! I am to start working at a 24-flat building in the next block from here," he explains as he comes home one day from the union steward's office.

"I begin March first so we can move out and have our own place."

"Wait till we tell my mother!" Aunt Justina explains happily. "Now she can come and live with us."

The apartment is in the basement; has two bedrooms, a dining room, living room and kitchen. One of the bedrooms is for Aunt Justina and Uncle Mike, the other will be for Aunt Theresia and me. Tobias will have to sleep on the couch in the living room.

Finally I have a room where I can study and share stories and secrets with Aunt Theresia as we lie in bed at night. At 14, I am beginning to notice boys at school and as most teens experience, there are always disappointments. The boys in my class are nice and helpful, but seem a little afraid to talk to me or approach me during the social events at school.

"There is one boy, very shy and not too smart in class, that seems drawn to me and I find myself enjoying his company. Although I have my eyes set on the really handsome boy in class, I see that he likes the best looking girl in class."

"That's how it goes, I guess," ponders Aunt Theresia as she listens to me. She is probably smiling in the darkness of the room, as she tries to console me.

"What should I do?" I question her.

"Just enjoy the company of the boys that like you. Don't wish for things you can't have."

The school year is slowly coming to an end, and in June 1950, I graduate from eighth grade. The ceremony is held at the church. We look very festive in light blue caps and gowns, marching in to the tune of "Pomp and Circumstance." I have done my best in school trying to learn English. I have overcome the language barrier, but need to learn much more of the seven years of grammar school I missed. Proudly I accept my diploma from Father Baron, the chaplain at our school. He always made a special point of praising me when he handed out the report cards. After the church ceremony and the congratulatory wishes from friends and family, a party follows in my honor. Our apartment is filled with decorations, food and well-wishers. I am very excited to be the center of attention.

I will be attending Aquinas Dominican High School, located right next to the grammar school. The teachers are also Dominican nuns. During the summer vacation I plan to study more history and English grammar so that I can keep up with my freshman class. Aunt Theresia helps me memorize names of each State, the presidents, and the dates of important history. I also read books from the library to catch up on the required reading. I don't understand everything, but at least I remember the titles and authors.

Though I don't see or hear from any of my classmates during the summer, I get together with two girls who also came from my hometown a few months before. Theresa and Mary are twins and used to live on my street in Gakowa. They are staying with their mother and grandparents. They live quite a distance from us, but we are able to walk to each other's houses. We don't have a car and the bus service is not convenient between the two places. We go to the movies on Saturdays or Sundays. We enjoy the cowboy movies, especially the ones starring Roy Rogers and Dale Evans. There are always two movies and a short subject, and the $1.00 allowance I get takes care of the movie and popcorn. Sometimes, Tobias gives me extra money to go to the movies again on Sunday.

When the girls and I return from the movies, we play games or talk about the boys we like, try out some make-up we borrow from their mother or dance with each other to the music on the radio. They are a lot of fun and we get along great.

When high school starts in the fall of 1950, I am prepared and enter my classes with great determination and joy. It's a new year, new uniforms, new nuns and new girls. It takes a while to get acquainted, but soon I join some clubs and activities that help bridge the gap. It's a beautiful school and there are many outlets for service. During lunch hour I volunteer to work at the supply store. We sell snacks and necessary school supplies.

The year ends with news about the immigration of my sister, Altmutter and the Findeis family. Uncle Mike has vouched for their housing and he has been promised a janitor's job for my uncle Anton. It will take some time for everything to be processed, but we trust that by summer of 1951, I will see my sister again. I wonder how much she has grown and if she remembers me. It will be fun to teach her English and show her Chicago. I know we will still be living with two different families, but we will see each other often and can talk on the telephone. I cannot wait till she comes!

High School and Beyond

A time to grow, a time to learn—I try my best!

It is January 1951, the beginning of the second half of my freshman year. The shiny floors in the halls of the Aquinas Dominican High School reflect my appearance like a mirror. I am on my way to the principal's office. A request from Sister Mary William is brought to my homeroom. I am wondering what she wants with me. I check my uniform. My starched white blouse is neatly tucked into my hunter green uniform skirt and the collar overlaps the suit jacket. There is nothing wrong with neither my white bobby socks nor the polished penny loafers. My nails are clean, my hair is combed and I don't wear make-up.

As soon as I enter the office, Sister comes out smiling and invites me into her private room. She asks me to sit down on the chair nearest her desk. Her hands are folded under her habit. Smiling, she says:

"Katherine, I must tell you that you failed the high school entrance exam last year."

I am shocked and tears begin to run down my cheeks. I lower my head so that Sister cannot see them. But with great determination, I look up and answer:

"But, Sister, you know that I just came from Germany a year ago."

Sister's hands come out from beneath her habit, gesturing firmly.

"Don't interrupt, Katherine, I am not finished. I am going to ask you to re-take the exam with the incoming freshman class, so that your school records will reflect the good work you are doing now."

With a sigh of relief I thank her and quickly leave the office. I am scheduled to try the exam again. When I return to my classroom, the girls whisper questions:

"What happened, Katherine?"

"I'll tell you later at lunchtime," I whisper back.

My friends gather around me while we eat lunch and I explain what Sister told me. They immediately offer to help me study for this test. Dorothy is great in social studies, Collette in science and Maureen in history.

"We could meet at Stineway's Drug store after school," they suggest. But I have to decline because it is my job to go home immediately after school to shop for the evening meal. While my aunt and uncle work, I am in charge of starting the supper.

"How about Saturday at the Library?" they counter.

I agree and am grateful for their enthusiasm. During these study sessions, they also want to know more about my life in Europe and my time in the concentration camp. I share some of my experiences with them, although I get emotional when trying to talk about it.

My mind wanders back to the town of Gakowa and I wonder where to start? Would they really be interested in all the horrible stories of my imprisonment in our own town, the hunger and illness, the loss of my mother and the absence of my father in the war? I begin with the story of my mother's death and my recovery from typhoid fever, and then continue with some of the happenings during the three years in the concentration camp. I leave out some of the details so as not to frighten them. I wonder if they really believe me because this part of history is little known.

The girls listen and express their sympathy on my loss. They are shocked by the many things that happened in a country far away. They wonder why no one knows about this.

Good news! Sister Mary William announces my passing of the test and congratulates me. I thank my friends whose help was crucial in this important endeavor.

I am the only foreign-born student at Aquinas. Although we all look alike in our uniforms, I feel my actions and German-accented words set me apart. The teachers and students treat me with special kindness and understanding. I study especially hard in the business classes. My typing and shorthand teachers are two little nuns who drill us mercilessly in daily competition. How many words can we type today? How many words per minute can we take in shorthand? It is hard but it will be my way to earn a living once I graduate. As much as I would like to go to college, my family cannot afford it. I probably cannot pass the college entrance exam, so I will ask the teachers to recommend me for a job in the secretarial field. Many corporations request Aquinas girls for their open positions at the end of the school year.

✳

It is August 1951. My cousin Tobias has been drafted into the army and will leave for assignment in Germany. At the same time, news of my sister's arrival in America coincides with Tobias' leaving. We all go to meet Aunt Barbara and Uncle Anton, Altmutter and Erna at Union Station in downtown Chicago. It has been two years since I saw Erna in Ludwigsburg and I wonder how much she has grown. She is now almost 10 years old. We will have to get reacquainted and I will have to teach her English.

The large train station is new to us and we have to ask Information about the train arrivals from New York. The hustle and bustle of the station is overwhelming and the loudspeaker's constant call of arrivals and departures confuses us. We finally find the right track and wait patiently for the arrival of the train.

Soon the locomotive glides into place; screeching wheels and billowing smoke announce the end of its journey. Now we all stretch our necks and turn our heads in different directions hoping to catch a glimpse of them. They will stand out among the regular American travelers, and they will be looking for us, too. The waiting is tense. Though we have waited for two years, we feel we cannot wait another minute.

A small girl is helped down the train steps by the conductor, followed by an elderly woman we recognize to be Altmutter. Now we race to them and help everyone else step down. This time, we can share happy tears of reunion, hugs and kisses and *Gruess Gott*—the usual welcome greeting familiar to us. Happy glances from other travelers remind us that we are making a scene, so we hurriedly find their baggage and return to the train station. Here, we have more room and can exchange greetings and news of their journey. While

Erna at age 11 with Altmutter and cousin Barbara Findeis in 1952.

the adults are busy talking, I ask Erna if she is hungry. She nods and I pull out a chocolate bar from my pocket. Her eyes widen as she opens the wrapping and takes a bite. She thanks me with her smiling eyes and says:

"Can you have chocolate anytime you want?"

"Not before dinner," I tell her, "but you will be surprised at all the things you can eat in America. You won't be hungry again."

Aunt Eva and Uncle Joe have come along to help transport everyone and their luggage back to our apartment. It will be crowded in our two-bedroom apartment with nine people. Sofas and rollaway beds in the living room and dining room come in handy at a time like this. But the promise of a janitor's job for Uncle Anton will provide a basement apartment for them.

Tobias must leave the next day, so he is anxious to talk to everyone and catch up on family news. We stay up late into the night because we cannot sleep with all the excitement. I hope that Erna and I will never be far apart again. We will live with two different families, but we can visit often.

Altmutter looks tired, yet she tells us about the journey. Their transportation was not as fast as ours. They came by boat to New York and then by train to Chicago. Erna is sleeping soundly in my bed, which we will share for the night. She looks frail and very shy to be in a new place again. Altmutter and Aunt Barbara assure me she is well and that she will adjust to being with me again.

After a short stay in our apartment, Altmutter, Erna and the Findeis Family move to a basement apartment which is supplied to the janitor of that building. Uncle Anton will be doing the janitor work, Aunt Barbara has found work cleaning houses, Cousin Barbara starts out in a factory and Altmutter takes care of the house.

The building they live in is too far away from our apartment for me to walk. Uncle Mike has a used car now, which he and Tobias bought with money they earned by doing vacation work for other janitors in the neighborhood. Sometimes they drive me to see Erna.

Erna and I talk on the phone and I keep up with her English lessons and try to help with her homework. On the weekends we see each other and, of course, on holidays and special occasions such as birthdays.

The people who live in the apartment above us, Mr. and Mrs. Culbertson, own a flower shop in downtown Chicago. They have no children and have taken a liking to me and Erna. Even though I am not yet 16 years old and unable to work legally, they ask me to help out in the store during the busy season. I water the plants, dust the shelves, and sweep the floor after Mrs. Culbertson finishes the flower arrangements. Sometimes I deliver corsages or vases of fresh flowers in the building where the shop is located. Often I receive tips, so I am happy to do this chore. I take the train downtown after school and must walk about five blocks to the shop. Luckily I get a ride home because we all live in the same building. I enjoy the hustle and bustle of the people walking in the streets, the cars honking and the elevated trains rumbling above.

Family celebrating Anton and Barbara Findeis' 25th wedding anniversary. Right to left: Erna, Kaethi, Altmutter, Barbara and Anton Findeis, Lisa Findeis (their daughter-in-law), Justina and Michael Brandt. Standing is John Findeis.

The Culbertsons are very kind to Erna. Often they take her to the flower shop too. Mrs. Culbertson is a fine American lady with blond hair and nice clothes. She always paints her fingernails red, which is something new to me. Since she has no children, Mrs. Culbertson asks if she can adopt Erna. Altmutter would not hear of it and declines her offer.

As time goes on, Mrs. Culbertson even teaches me to arrange flowers and make corsages. I like working with the fragrant roses, the violet-colored orchids, the long-stemmed gladiolas and the colorful birds-of-paradise.

Even though the girls at school are friendly and helpful, no one invites me to their homes or to any parties. I, in turn, am too shy to invite them to our apartment. So I spend a lot of time either working or with other young people who have immigrated to Chicago. Some of our cousins have arrived, as well as friends from our town of Gakowa. My aunt and uncle join the adults in weekly Saturday night card games. I spend my time at home. It is a lonely time for me. I am not yet old enough to go out by myself in the evenings. I listen to music on the record player that I was given for Christmas. I have always loved our folk songs and brass music, which we can buy in the German music stores on the north side of Chicago. I also have a passion for dancing. I cannot sit still when a waltz or polka is being played.

I also like to write. I write poems and short stories in German. To illustrate the stories, I cut out pictures from magazines and make little booklets. One of the poems reflects my thoughts of Gakowa and what has happened to my hometown.

Es war einmal	*Once upon a time*
Das Dorf ist leer	*The town is empty*
Die Felder kahl,	*The fields are barren*
Der Kirchhof ist ein Traenental	*The cemetery is a valley of tears*
Die stolzen Mauern Truemmer sind	*The proud houses are in ruins*
Befreundet nur mit Sonn' und Wind	*Their only friends are the sun and the wind*
Schon viele Jahre ist es her	*It has been many years since then*
Das Lager war, doch ist nicht mehr	*The camp existed but is no more*
Doch trotzdem senden uns die Sterne	*And yet, the stars send us*
Heimatgruesse in die Ferne	*Greetings from home to the distant lands*

(Special Note: In 1991 this poem was published in a German magazine called *Der Schwengelbrunnen.*)

———————— ✳ ————————

Sophomore year in high school is coming to an end and I am looking for a full time summer job now that I am 16 years old. Betty, a friend of mine who lives nearby, also from Gakowa, tells me about a job that she has applied for at a major printing company. She

Barbara and Anton Findeis, 1952.

encourages me to apply as well. We take the Illinois Central train to R.R. Donnelly & Company, near downtown Chicago. The train stops right in front of the place.

We go to the personnel office and ask for an application. I also ask what type of jobs there are available for me.

"Don't worry; you'll be able to do this work," the office manager informs me. "You will be collating pages of catalogs we are working on right now. It is a job where you will stand all day."

I can see that the printing shop is in a big building but the windows are open, so there will be no air conditioning. No doubt it will be hot inside. I also ask about pay and am told that $1.00 per hour is starting salary. I quickly calculate that to be $40.00 a week.

The following Monday, Betty and I board the train leaving from 71st and Jeffery and are on our way to work. We are given our places to stand in a row of collating boxes and wait for the clerks to bring us the printed pages. Stacks of paper are in front of me waiting to be inserted into the correct page numbers of the catalog. It is boring work and very repetitive, but we are obligated to do a certain number of pages each day. If we go over, there will be a bonus on our check. Unfortunately, I am never able to pass my quota.

At break time, my feet hurt so badly that I just sit on the floor and rest. On certain days, when the heat is particularly unbearable, we spray our faces with cool water in the bathroom. On the way home, the train is also not air conditioned. The windows are open but are not giving us the cool breeze we expect.

At 16, I am not used to working this hard. When I come home, there is not much more I want to do but take a cool shower and sit on the couch. Uncle Mike and Aunt Justina work so hard all day that I am ashamed to admit how tired I am, but I am not used to this. The train fare and some money for the movies take some of my pay, but I open a savings account and am proud to add some of the hard-earned money each week.

--------------------- ✳ ---------------------

It is March 1953, and a letter from Hoeger Oma, my father's mother, arrives in an envelope with a black border. I see it lying on the hall table when I come home from school. A black border usually indicates a death, and in my heart I already know that another family member is gone. It is Opa.

I call Erna to tell her the sad news. She hardly remembers him— it's been six years since we left Gakowa, and she was only a little girl of six then.

"Opa is buried in the cemetery in Sombor, and now Oma doesn't know what she is going to do," I say.

"Can she come here?" Erna asks.

"I don't think so. She wants to go to Germany, but first she would have to buy out her citizenship in Yugoslavia, and it would cost a lot of money."

"Oma wants to know what we think she should do," I continue. "I believe she will receive a pension from the German government because our father served in the army and has been declared missing in action."

We both agree it would be best if she left Yugoslavia. After I hang up the phone, I sit down and write a letter to Oma and enclose some money which I had saved from working in the flower shop during the summer.

--------------------- ✳ ---------------------

It's been two years since Tobias left for the army. The time for his release is near and in a letter he tells us that he will be home soon. When he arrives, a welcome home party with all the relatives is planned. Since he left, many more cousins and aunts and uncles have come to Chicago. He is surprised to see so many new faces and it is a happy day. Aunt Justina has cooked some sausages and sauerkraut and baked a cake. The other relatives bring homemade cookies. We all crowd into the basement apartment where we live and enjoy Tobias' return home.

"While I was in the army, the boys called me "Toby", he informs us, "so why don't you call me that from now on."

"I think that's more American," I conclude, "and it's a shorter name."

There are many social activities for the German immigrants on the north side of Chicago. Dances are held in the Lincoln Turner hall and the young people meet there on Saturday nights. Soon Toby tells us that he met a girl named Anna, who was also in a Russian labor camp like him. She happens to live close to our apartment on Bennett Avenue. I guess they have a lot in common and at Christmas 1953, he announces their engagement to be married the following July.

How excited I am! This will be the first family wedding. The wedding and my high school graduation will be close together so there will be much to do.

The final months in my senior year at Aquinas High School are full of activities. There are concerts, Flag Day celebration, scholarship award ceremonies, the final moments of choosing colleges or jobs and of course, the graduation.

As has been the custom for all special occasions, the graduation is held in the church just a few steps away from the school. In white caps and gowns we seniors march in single file to the music of "Pomp and Circumstance." The nuns, who have taught us the past four years, follow the graduates. Each girl has her eyes on the pews where her relatives are seated. Smiles radiate from each face, proud and confident. I slide into the pew assigned to me. I feel proud of my accomplishments and look forward to my new job which has been arranged for me by my teachers. My mind wanders during the ceremony while I imagine how far I have come in my eighteen years of life. So much has happened, yet I have been blessed.

"Katherine Hoeger, congratulations," the principal calls out as I walk proudly up the steps to the altar to receive my diploma.

After this final event in the school year, we leave the church with a joyous feeling of freedom. We hug and say our goodbyes, promising to keep in touch but knowing we probably won't. I thank the nuns and the girls for the many hours of special attention and help I received from them during the last four years. They, in turn, wish me well.

"Just keep on typing like you've been doing," Sister Ethel encourages me, as she pats me on the shoulder. "I know you'll do us proud."

My new job will be in the steno pool at a large corporation, where I can put my typing and shorthand to good use. I am a little nervous about taking dictation, wondering if I can keep up. Time and experience will be my new teacher.

It's been a time for learning and growing up. I leave with a little sadness because now I am destined to work for the rest of my life, but I look forward to it.

Soon after the graduation, the wedding of Toby and Anna is nearing. On July 3rd they are married in the same church in which I graduated. I am one of the bridesmaids, all decked out in a long formal gown. Erna has a new dress as well. The wedding is celebrated in the traditional custom of our German heritage. One of the customs of our people is the *bridal dance*; each person pays for the privilege of dancing with the bride. Then at midnight, the bridal veil is removed and replaced with a headscarf and an apron is tied around the "new housewife." The groom has to watch out so that the boys don't steal the bride because he will have to pay to get her back. Among the usual waltzes and polkas, the guests sing their favorite old time folksongs. The festivities are a welcome change from the hard work that the janitors and maids perform each day. This is a chance for them to dance, to sing and be merry. Tomorrow would be another day of hard work.

The reception is in a banquet hall large enough to accommodate the many relatives and friends. All the children are invited too and they have a wonderful time. It is a family gathering and the bartenders are some of the wedding guests. They take turns serving the drinks. The festivities continue late into the night and at midnight, a snack of homemade sausages, pickled peppers, rye bread and more homemade cookies are spread out on the banquet tables. There seems to be no curfew and the music only stops when the morning begins to dawn.

I am exhausted from dancing the polkas and waltzes all evening and fall into bed dreaming of my own wedding some day.

Toby and Anna move into an apartment in a building where he will be working as janitor. This will be the first time Toby will have a private bedroom since he left Gakowa, ten years ago.

My daily train ride to my job in the secretarial pool at Americana Corporation becomes routine as I watch other riders and the scenery passing me by. I often think about my life in the concentration camp and the writer in me starts to jot down memories in a journal during the train ride to and from work. Words become sentences and sentences become paragraphs as my heart pours out my inner most feelings of my time there. Things that I never talked about or feelings hidden deep in my soul, come out on these pages. Often I feel tears running down my cheeks as I remember the many frightful things that happened to me. I quickly wipe them away and look up to see if anyone has noticed.

In the office, there are four girls who take dictation from various bosses in the company. A maiden lady, Miss Zimmer, who looks much like my teacher in Germany, is in charge of the department. She is a friend of the head of the Educational Department, Miss Goldstein, and sends me to take her dictation. Miss Goldstein, a Jewish lady, who is familiar with the Jewish Holocaust, is very kind to me. She is very interested in my experiences and very protective of me when we work with the heavy metal file boxes in which the records of the country's schools are kept.

"Don't you lift these heavy boxes," she worries, "or you'll hurt yourself and never be able to have children."

I smile and thank her for her concern, but don't know what that has to do with having children. She always calls one of the male workers to help us. I enjoy working for her because she is more of a mother than a boss to me. We often discuss the Jewish Holocaust in comparison to my experiences. She wants to know what happened to me and my family and it's gratifying to know someone cares.

Several other girls who graduated from Aquinas High School in previous years, work there also. We get to be friends, have lunch and sometimes go to the show after work. But, on the ride home on the train, I get out the journal and continue my writings. Soon I have many pages and begin to type them to prepare a booklet.

In September 1954, it is five years since we arrived in America. It is time to apply for citizenship. Uncle Mike, Aunt Justina and Toby are called first because their name begins with a B. I must wait a little longer and it takes until March 1955, for my papers to come through. Two witnesses are required so Miss Zimmer and Miss Goldstein volunteer to come with me. We interrupt our work day and go to City Hall. We take a taxi which is new to me. I have never been on a taxi ride. I am a little nervous because there is a test about the history of the United States and the workings of the government. When we arrive, I am ushered into a room with other immigrants who will be taking the test. Miss Zimmer and Miss Goldstein are directed to the waiting room.

"Katherine, good luck," they call out to me, "just do the best you can."

When I look at the questionnaire, I am relieved to find that most of this information is fresh in my mind from High School. When I finish the questionnaire, I leave the room with a smile and feel content that I passed. Miss Zimmer and Miss Goldstein come back into the room and are questioned by the clerk about my character and if I would make a good American citizen. They give me a glowing report and we are done. Relieved, I thank them and we go out to lunch to celebrate this special day. We then take a taxi back to work. A vase of flowers awaits me on my desk when we return—a token of congratulations from my co-workers.

A swearing-in ceremony for the prospective citizens will follow later, but I feel like an American already.

———————————— ✳ ————————————

In the fall of 1954, Uncle Mike is offered another janitor job at a high rise building on South Shore Drive in Chicago. It's a better job, but the apartment has only one bedroom. We will make do. Aunt Theresia and I get to sleep in the bedroom and Uncle Mike and Aunt Justina buy a sleeper sofa for the living room. The kitchen is small and there is not much closet space, but the view is great. We look out onto Rainbow Park, and it is only a few hundred yards to Lake Michigan and the beach. It seems like we are on vacation every day. Soon we prepare for the Christmas holidays and my 19th birthday. Since we live in a new neighborhood, it is hard for me to meet young people my age. Most of the graduation class is off to college and I can only keep in touch with some of the girls by mail.

Altmutter and Erna and the Findeis family have also moved to another apartment not too far away from us. Erna attends 7th grade now and is doing well in school. In order to make more room for the family in the small apartment, Altmutter takes a job as a housekeeper in a Catholic Church rectory. She is able to live there all week and receives her meals along with a salary. At age 63, this is an admirable undertaking. While there, she learns English from the priests and also studies to become a citizen. She tries very hard to learn to write and practices in a notebook usually used by grade school children. We are very proud of her. She wants to become an American citizen. In her desire to preserve some of the experiences in the concentration camp, she also keeps a record of some of the facts she deems important, such as deaths of family members and some of the important dates that are vital to our family history. This, of course, is written in German in a very simple script.

Some of the cousins who have arrived recently ask me to accompany them to the German dances held on the north side of Chicago. It is difficult to get there with public transportation, but we finally figure it out. We take a bus, then the elevated train and arrive very close to the dance hall. The Lincoln Turner hall is the favorite place of the young immigrants. It takes quite a while to get there and it is very late at night when we return. The walk home by myself from the bus station is a little scary for me. It is most likely still the fear I have not overcome from my years in the camp. When I get off the bus, I run all the way home and breathe a sigh of relief when I close my front door.

On one occasion, while enjoying the dance music and the camaraderie of a table full of friends, something special happened. I love to dance, so when one young man asks me, I am happy to join him.

"You're a good dancer, Katherine," a friend, Frank, tells me. "Where did you learn it?"

"Thank you, Frank, but I've always liked to dance, it's in my blood. When I hear a waltz or a polka, my heart skips a beat. I can't sit still, when I hear music."

The music stops and Frank and I are breathless from the fast tempo of the polka.

"Let's sit down, I need something cool to drink," I tell Frank.

The dance hall is crowded and when I return to the table, someone is sitting in my chair. I am a little upset at losing my seat. I tap the young man on the shoulder.

"Excuse me, you are in my seat," I tell him rather harshly. He turns around, smiles from ear to ear, a strand of his dark hair on his forehead, and says:

"Hello, I am George, may I have this dance?"

The
Homecoming

Τ he paths that led two children from their homes in Gakowa
and Bezdan, Yugoslavia through years of hardships and many
towns and cities, had finally crossed in Chicago. But, though
many years had passed, they could not forget their homeland. They had to
go back to see what, if anything, remained.

It is a warm and sunny day in September 2003, and I am standing
in front of the house in which I was born in Gakowa, Yugoslavia. It is
in abominable shape. The roof has holes in it, the walls are chipped, the
doors and windows hang crookedly in their frames, and the fence around
the garden has been torn down. I look for the cherry trees in the garden and
the chestnut trees that once graced the side of the house. They are gone.

The street is empty and quiet. Tears trickle down my cheeks, and
my heart aches. My husband, George, who is standing next to me,
takes my arm to comfort me.

A little girl, riding her bicycle along the sidewalk, notices us and
goes inside to call her mother. The lady of the house comes out and
invites us in. She speaks only Serbian so we cannot communicate.
However, I place my hands on my heart and point to the house, and
she seems to understand that I once lived here.

She guides us into the house through the weathered and broken
door. Once inside, we enter the gangway which will lead to the living quarters. I step up into the room that once was the bedroom of
my grandparents. It is dark and dusty. Clothes are piled up in a cor-

Sketch of our birthplace in Gakowa, as it was in 1944.
(Sketch by Matthew Sesek)

ner, and there is no furniture except for a television. I then go into my parents' bedroom. When I see the room I was born in and where my mother died, I am overcome with memories.

"There was a desk in that corner where my father sat and worked in the evenings," I tell George. "My mother used to help him with the bookkeeping and Erna would play on the floor. My bed was over here. I slept with a down blanket, and there was a tiled oven in the corner. Even in the winter, it was warm."

"Does anything look familiar to you now?" he asks.

"No," I say. "I can't believe this was once my home."

The missing plaster on the ceiling and walls, the filthy floor, boxes strewn all over the place, reminds me that this house has been neglected for a long time. I don't know how long this lady has been living here, so I cannot blame her for the condition of this house.

We walk into the back yard. A literal pigsty greets us with overgrown weeds surrounding a couple of old cars and chickens pecking the ground for food. A caged piglet squeals at us from the open slats of his corral. I am heartbroken to see that the doors to our kitchen and my mother's sewing room are hanging from their hinges, bro-

Photo of the Hoeger house in Gakowa, 2003.

ken and weathered. It resembles a place that has been totally neglected over the past 55 years.

The well is surrounded by weeds and some bricks are missing.
Is anyone using it? I can still see my mother dipping a cup into the
bucket for fresh water. This is almost too much for me to bear. I am
numb. This once beautiful place has been totally destroyed.

We wander slowly towards the front gate but before we reach it,
the lady gestures to George that he should take a photograph of her
and me. She seems genuinely sorry for our disappointment. I take a
small pebble from the garden and a chestnut from under the last tree.
These will be my treasures to keep. This short visit convinces me that
this is no longer my home, it is just a memory. We stand and take a
last look. It is no longer ours, but the nine years I spent here with my
family is enough to hold in my heart forever. After all, it is not the
brick and mortar that makes up a home; it is the people in it.

We walk down the *Bahnhofstrasse,* named after the railroad station across the street from my home. The street is paved now and
some of the houses have been renovated and painted. I have the
eerie feeling that the people inside are looking out at us. But in my

mind I see our friendly neighbors and my friends playing on the sidewalk, skipping rope. I see my mother pushing the baby buggy with my sister in it, while I am walking by her side. I see some horse-drawn wagons loaded with the harvested beets and potatoes. I see my hometown as it was many years ago before the terrible war.

At the end of the Bahnhofstrasse is the cemetery. We have come to find my mother's grave. Through many years of neglect, tall grasses and thorn bushes have become interwoven so tightly that one cannot see through them. The thorns seem to warn us not to come closer; but we have come so far and cannot give up this easily. George has tried to penetrate the bushes with his arms.

"I am sorry, Katherine, but I can't get through," he calls from the bushes. "My hands and arms are bleeding."

"Well, you tried," I assure him, "we can always put the flowers on top of the bushes."

George throws the bouquet in the direction of my mother's grave and it is perched facing heavenward. We hope she will see it and know we were here. Being here so close to our loved ones, lying among this field of thorns, helps to relieve our need to have done something.

A silent prayer, directed to the God watching over us, asks that our efforts are not in vain.

In the fenced-in, grassy field behind the cemetery are the mass graves of the concentration camp victims. On this hallowed ground lie the innocent children who starved to death, the old people who died of malaria and typhoid fever, and the victims of abuse and firing squads. It is a barren sight. There are about 8,000 people buried here without any dignity or markers. It is the burial ground of George's grandmother as well.

As we continue onto Main Street, the weather has changed and a slow drizzle begins to fall. With umbrella and camera in hand we continue north towards the old school and the site of the church that was destroyed in 1970. We look into the windows of the old school, its building shabby and the stucco crumbling. There are people living in the building and a new school stands behind the old. We see the children playing ball during recess, as we had done so many years before. I attended only two years of school in this building before it all ended. Although it's been many years, I can remember the names and faces of some of my classmates.

Our visit to the Memorial in Gakowa, Yugoslavia in 2003—dedicated to the
thousands of victims in the death camp "Gakowa" during 1944–1948.

Going further north on Main Street, we pass the houses of my aunts and uncles and my grandparents. As a child, I visited here often. So many memories come back...

The holiday visits, the summer vacations spent here during the harvesting of the grapes in grandfather's vineyard, the picking of the apples and berries, the festivals in the church.

I try not to think of the many horrendous things that happened on this street and in those houses while we were incarcerated here, but it's hard to forget the partisans marching two by two, their boots clicking, their rifles always ready to shoot. It was a nightmare to see the wagons loaded with corpses being pushed towards the mass graves by inmates who might soon be on that wagon themselves.

The rain has stopped and the sun peeks out, imitating the way that life's journey changes. We have come home to see and touch our legacy.

Epilogue

In February 1957 George and I were married. Our son, Peter, was born a year later. At that time, my Hoeger Oma came for a visit. She helped with the baby while I worked. Two years later, our daughter, Heide Marie, was born. By this time, Oma had to return to Germany because she had come on a visitor's visa. She wanted very much to stay here with us. It was difficult to get a permanent visa for a Yugoslavian born person. We tried various government offices, but were finally directed to Senator Wm. Langer, of North Dakota, who helped pass a Private Bill for Oma to remain in this country. The bill was passed by the Senate, House of Representatives and President Eisenhower. She was here to stay.

George left his work as a butcher and became a janitor like all our relatives on the South Side of Chicago. In 1967, our second daughter, Katherine Ann, was born to complete the family. Oma lived to her 81st birthday.

Erna married Matthew Sesek, an immigrant from Slovenia, in 1965. Twin sons, Robert and Richard, arrived in 1966. Matthew is a commercial artist and started his own successful business. He is the artist on the book cover. Their sons are married, and their grandchildren, Tony, Anabel and Hugo are their pride and joy.

Altmutter retired from the rectory and was able to attend Erna and Matt's wedding before passing away at age 75. The Findeis family also lived near us. Uncle Anton died in 1978 at the age of 85 and

Aunt Barbara is now 93 years old and living in an assisted-living facility. Their daughter Barbara married Wade Minster in 1958 and they have a daughter, Nancy.

Uncle Mike and Aunt Justina lived near us and enjoyed our children like any "grandparents" would. Their son, Tobias and his wife, Anna, have one daughter, Rosemary. Uncle Mike died in 1988 and Aunt Justina died in 1990. Aunt Theresia lived with them until her death at the age of 92.

George's parents retired to Wonder Lake, IL. His father died at age 81 and his mother lived to be 95 years old. His brother, Larry, married but was widowed after ten years of marriage, leaving him with three small children. He also lived in Wonder Lake and with the help of his parents, raised the children. He has remarried just recently to Vivian, a widow, and they live in Wisconsin. The youngest brother, John, married in 1961 and a son, John Jr. was born in 1962. Unfortunately, an incurable disease at the time, uremic poisoning, took his brother's life in 1963.

Our lives have been full. Our five grandchildren, Dan, Lynne, Clay, Cole and Marin are the final legacy of this story.

The Sunsets of my Life...

As evening bows its head to earth
And stillness fills the air
One sees the splendor in the sky.

As a child I asked my mother why
The sky turns red and gold.
She told me with a loving smile,
Behold!
And you will see the face of God

And then my mother died...
I saw the sunset through my tears
And asked God—why?
He said: Beyond the sunset is her home

Times changed; hunger, pain and fear
Were always near.
I still loved the sunset
And God said: I am always with you

I escaped and walked to freedom
The journey long and hard
The sunset was my only joy
And God said: I am walking right behind you

As I grew up and learned to love
The many sunsets in my life
I marveled at the glorious sight
And God said: This is my gift to you

ACKNOWLEDGEMENTS

To my husband, George, whose keen memory can recall the smallest details about his life, the history of World War II and the traditions of the Donauschwaben in Yugoslavia.

To the writings of Father Wendelin Gruber, author of "In The Claws of the Red Dragon" from whose pages I refreshed my memory about the concentration camp Gakowa, where he ministered to the inhabitants.

To Elisabeth Walter, author of "Barefoot in the Rubble," who has been a staunch friend and mentor. She encouraged me and gave me the final push to write this book.

To Dr. Ignatz Stein, who documented the history of the town of Gakowa, and the details of the concentration camp's beginning in the "Ortissippenbuch Gakowa."

To all the members of my writers groups "Writer's Expression" and "Write On Hoosiers," who listened to my story. Their critique is beyond measure.

ABOUT THE AUTHOR

KATHERINE HOEGER FLOTZ
wrote this book in her mind many years
ago. She documented portions of her
memories after high school graduation
in 1954. The manuscript found a place
in her dresser drawer until she was questioned by her children about her childhood.

All through the years, she has been involved with keeping alive the
memories of her experiences, those of her husband's, and of other
Donauschwaben friends. For forty years, she has been the secretary of the
Batschka Club, a social club of *Donauschwaben* from Gakowa, Kruschiwl,
and other surrounding towns.

She considers her writing abilities a gift, and feels she overcame all
her ordeals so that she could write this book.

The timing of this book is exactly 60 years after the start of the concentration camp. Why did she wait this long to write it? Working to
raise and educate their three children was her priority. Now that the
job is done, the writing of this book became her passion.

She feels that not only was *her* story important to tell, but also that
of her husband's. They co-authored—she took their collective memories and put them into words. Their collaboration worked well.
The book is a labor of love for their children and grandchildren. It
was written for them, for all the children and grandchildren of the
Donauschwaben who never lived to tell about it, and all people who
have experienced oppression, abuse and loss of their freedom.